JACK WEST FUNERAL DIRECTOR

Self and Daphne — A London Banquet

JACK WEST FUNERAL DIRECTOR

Jack West

ARTHUR H. STOCKWELL LTD.
Elms Court   Ilfracombe
Devon

ISBN 0 7223 2287-9
Printed in Great Britain by
Arthur H. Stockwell Ltd.
Elms Court   Ilfracombe
Devon

CONTENTS

LIST OF ILLUSTRATIONS

PREFACE

With my very active life of work and business commitments all of which have been so rewarding, time has seemed all too scarce to read a book, let alone write one.

Yet having arrived at a state of semi-retirement, with the opportunity to leave most of the day to day responsibilities to Jeremy and his staff, I have through the last few years, at home and while holiday cruising, away from it all, been able to collect together many of my memories and thoughts of the past years. And with Jacqui's help in typing and the experience of my publishers, I have been able to present the various chapters of my life with the sincere hope that readers will find them interesting and perhaps inspiring.

I would thank Daphne for her help and encouragement to produce such an informative book, foremost for our children and grandchildren, that they may learn something of what I have been able to do with the various opportunities that have been offered to me all through my life.

Everything I have written in my simple way of telling a story is entirely factual. I have added nothing to glamorise any experience that has been responsible to lead me on to obtain that which I set out to do through good health, hard work and trying never to waste time, material and opportunity.

Jack West

EARLY YEARS

Although I have only been told about it, my imagination allows me to picture the scene that took place on the 2nd September 1910. Soon after my entry into this world, all ten pounds of me was held up to the bedroom window of The White House, on a towel, to greet who was eventually to become my favourite workman, Jack Collard. He was arriving on his own birthday, to start his day's work for my father as a bricklayer. I am sure that this had some influence to call me Jack instead of John as my father and grandfather were named.

My earliest memory was to have entered my mother's bedroom and watch my younger brother taking his nourishment. She was cuddling him in bed, I was not envious, for I accepted that it was my pleasure when I needed it.

Nothing more remained with me, until I acquired a surplus of energy. My father, a builder, surrounded by yard and workshop, decided to give my mother some relief during the hot summer days, by making up a play-pen in the yard, upon an old carpet, where I could rake around with a few toys and upset no one, and would be quite safe. I am told that I acquired such a tan, that folks questioned my parents as to whether they had adopted a 'half-caste'. As I became independent of such limitation, my brother and I would avail ourselves of the things around the yard that would respond to our imagination. We found it possible to arrange the scaffold boards to produce an aeroplane that we could sit in and pretend to use the controls. I am not sure whether we returned them to the store or left them for my father to clear away.

Now five or six years old, the First World War had brought

Age 2 years with my brother and sister

The White House, Rainham Road South, Dagenham — demolished 1966

its austerity. The workman had left for the forces, and my father's partner, Mr Coe had been directed to Hatfield, for carpenters were needed to produce aeroplanes. Food became a problem to satisfy the family, now one girl and four healthy boys.

We all lived together in The White House, a large old five-bedroomed farmhouse with a cellar, that we used as a shelter. On the night of an air raid in 1916 we were all got up to witness an L1 Robbinson VC attack and bring down the German Zeppelin loaded with bombs for London. The gleaming fragments dropped from the sky as we could see our planes zooming in and out of the searchlights; apart from this we were saved from the real excitement of war.

My mother like most, would deny themselves of good nutritious food for the sake of the growing children. Although we had a large bath upstairs, there was no hot-water system, or safe room heating in the winter, which meant heating the water in the scullery copper that was fired with solid fuel. A large round galvanized bath would be placed on the hearthrug, my sister would be the first to be cleaned, and we boys would follow with a little added hot water. A fairly serious affair to avoid splashing the surrounding carpets. It was usually a Saturday night treat. I am sure my parents who shared the job, must have been tired when the performance was over, and all were in bed.

My mother did have the help of Nan Flack who never failed to arrive at about the eighth month with her little black bag. She would perform all that was neccessary to start another 'little West' on the road to a long and healthy life, she would also revisit for a little after-care, to help my mother with all that she had to cope with.

It was long before the introduction of brightly-coloured packets of breakfast cereals, for often our bread and milk would receive extra appetizers, by cutting the bread into shapes of ships and bridges to float around the dish of milk, an inevitable part of our daily diet. With the farm only a short walking distance, it became an accepted job for one of us to pick up the tall blue enamel can, that had a lid fitted to form a mug.

On arriving home from school we would wait outside the farmhouse door for the fresh warm milk to be brought in from the cow-shed. Most of the time it was returned without spilling it, although there was the odd occasion when it was frosty or that we would swing it round with the lid off to show off and spill some, that would result in something that would remind us to be more careful next time.

As a family we were well provided for in every way, we were blessed with ideal parents, even if we did not entirely appreciate them at all times. We were brought up in close contact with the Methodist Church, which was directly opposite our house, for we all attended Sunday school. My grandmother was a long and respected member, quite proud that her grandchildren were taking an active part, except of course for the odd occasion. One Sunday morning the organist left the organ to take me out for being a 'noisy little fidget', but I was soon back in the fold, for the organist's daughter Gus took me under her wing and subsequently made a lifelong friend of me. I continued as a teacher and steward and in membership all my life.

As time went on I tried to understand John Wesley's experience, ''To work as hard as you can, Earn as much money as you can, Give as much away as you can''. On the first two counts I feel I have succeeded, but I know I could do more in return for the happy childhood my parents offered.

One day on returning home from school we found an old horse-drawn coach in the yard, my father had purchased it from the local job master. The wheels had to be returned, but it was set up in the yard as a little house for us boys, we called it 'The Cabin'. We would invite our mates in to exchange our cigarette cards or select our football team, and at times, we'd set up the front to work the ratchet brake, and with wild imagination a proper 'Wells Fargo'.

My father lacked nothing to provide us with entertainment. On another occasion he converted our old wooden mail-cart (pram) that had seen the five of us through our dependent stage into a swing-boat that we could sit in together. When my sister became old enough he bought her a second-hand girl's bike and taught her to ride, by running alongside and supporting the frame. After a time we boys all learned to ride it, until it became anybody's bike for even the shortest run, around the corner for a two and half penny loaf of bread, and when we would require it later on in the day, we would work out by deduction, that it was left round outside Arthy's shop. Sure enough there it was, nobody had touched it. On a Saturday morning with boiled rice for lunch, our treat would be to pop round to Arthy's between the courses for seven for 3½d jam puffs.

On a Sunday morning my father would take it upon himself to prepare the breakfast, fried bread and gravy with celebrated sausages purchased the day before, from Axons in the high street at Romford. A little shop that would sell pigs' trotters and 'chidlings', steaming hot late on a Saturday night.

Christmas was always a happy time, we had plenty of rooms, one a living-room which had a large solid walnut dining-table, a chair at each end, two on one side and three on the serving side. The family of seven always sat in the same places. My mother and father, as many other large families in the village, found time to fill each hung up stocking with a few sweets, small toys and usually a torch to discover what 'He' had left, early in the morning. We would come down full of excitement, have our breakfast, then to be sent into the parlour, while mum and dad arranged all the larger presents they had for us, also those sent in by aunts and uncles. They would be piled on the table in our places, then covered with a large cloth, to be removed when we were all seated, thus we would all be so absorbed in our own as not to be envious of each other's.

The large house lent itself to parties of relations, and a week or two later we had a party for our mates. We were permitted to invite two or three each. This necessitated setting up a large table in the scullery, a long room across the back of the house, with a floor of stone slabs. When the knocker would start about five o'clock, we five would be really excited to welcome our own mates, until my parents had found that their family had grown to twenty or more, many from families where their cottages consisted of two small rooms downstairs, and two small bedrooms to accommodate eight, ten or even twelve children. Our house was renowned for its Christmas parties.

We were also privileged with a large yard and a workshop with its floor covered with crisp wood shavings to romp about in, and be temped to try out the carpenter's planes, only to be reprimanded for damaging the edges.

I could only have been about three years old, when I wandered out into the workshop and pulled a pail of boiling pitch over, that had been prepared to line a coffin. I have no memory of it, except what my parents told me, that my

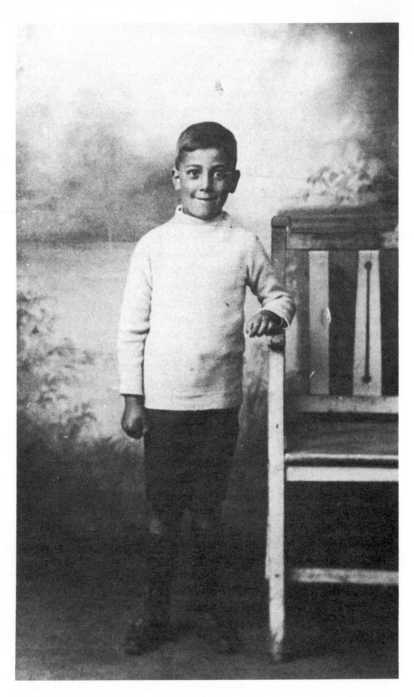

Age 8 years

condition of the scald matted my curls to my face, and gave them great anxiety. Doctor Prosser Evans the local doctor was called to at least save my life, if not my face from a lifelong scar, which of course I am not conscious of, unless I look in a mirror. In recent years I have accepted it as an initiation or brand, since I am the only one of my family to have accepted the calling of the funeral trade.

As we four boys grew up together, with only about five to six years separating the youngest from the eldest, we were permitted to mix with all other children in the street, some were very poor. On returning home from school they would be handed a large sandwich of bread and jam then sent out to play, leaving room for the elder brothers and sisters to be seated at the table, on their return from work. Sleeping I was assured was only possible to sleep four or five in a bed, end to end, and yet these children survived and grew into worthy citizens. We would play such street games as 'Tin Can Copper' or 'Release'. Our street widened out by 'The Bull' as it joined Rookery Farm, managed by the Maddocks family. It was on this setting void of any motor taffic in those days, that we could mark out an area by laying down our coats. One would remain within the den, while the others would hide away until they were caught and parked within the den with others, to be released by some bright kid who could run through while the guard was out seeking others. During our game there would be a distraction, Mr Maddocks would leave the farm every evening about five o'clock to drive his trap down to the railway station, with two churns of milk and leave it on the platform to be taken by steam train to Plaistow Hospital. We were allowed to sit on the back for a ride. On return we may have spotted the 'straw carts', a convoy of possibly six or seven single horse carts loaded high with loose straw gathered from Aveley and beyond, by dealers returning to Becontree Heath for resale to London stables. We would take the opportunity to pull some straw from the last cart as the driver was hidden by his large load, such we would require for our chickens.

Alongside our workshop my father stored lengths of timber and scaffold poles etc. Apart from the general use, there would be occasions when men of the village would assist him to load the poles etc. onto the handcart for erecting side-shows and coconut shies on the vicarage field which was owned by the church, and provided the main field for outside entertainment. We boys would enter into such excitement in these events. My father also held the responsibility of what was known as the 'parish chairs', some hundred or so cane chairs that were stored in a loft in the Fords School, to be hired out to any event that required them for a small charge to cover replacements. He would expect one of us boys to help hand them down, often on a Saturday afternoon.

My father's firm was responsible for the parish church maintenance. About 1913 they took on the mammoth task of completely reroofing the nave of the church. This required a scaffold and platform mounted to work from. A photograph shows the vicar Rev Harrison with his curate Rev G. Jones and churchwarden, also my father and his workman; it no doubt was work to be proud of, for my brother and I were taken up to be pictured with my favourite workman. I was told that Mr Vargo Williams was responsible for obtaining the very large pine timber, visible in the roof. I was about eleven years old, when the firm accepted the job to dismantle the church steeple, for it was found to be infested with dry rot. So soon after the war, the repair bill would have been impossible for the village folk to have met.

My father subcontracted to a firm of steeplejacks, to remove the copper weather-vane from the top and dismantle the copper-faced timber structure. On my way home from school one summer afternoon I called in, if only to be introduced to the steeplejacks by Jack Collard. They must have taken to the governor's son, for they offered me a ride up the outside of the tower in a 'Palmers Cradle'. Having reached the base of the steeple, they kidded me to climb the almost straight ladder to the very top with the assurance of one in front of me and one behind, it was a terrific sensation feeling the near straight ladder would pull out to let me fall. They must have been sure of what risk they were taking with the governor's son. When I descended glowing with excitement, having done it, they cut off the highest point of the lightning-conductor as a souvenir and handed it to me, I scratched the date on it, June 1921. I believe I am somewhat saddened at losing it through the years.

The base was felted over, and a flagstaff erected. For several

*Reroofing Dagenham Parish Church — Rev Harrison, Vicar; Rev G. Jones, Curate;
my father and his workman. Myself extreme right in Jack Collard's arms*

A school photo about 11 years

Dagenham Parish Church 1921;

Steeplejacks at work

years the vicar would instruct my father to hoist a flag on special occasions, and he would take me up inside the tower to help him.

Very few folk were ever able to have an annual holiday, and so a day out was a real event. As Sunday school children, there was always the annual Sunday school treat at Southend, of which we were expected to pay some small amount towards the fare and tea.

On Friday evening we would collect our tie-on label from the schoolroom, on this would be the local school stamp and times to meet, first at 8.30 a.m. at the hall roll call, prayers for a happy day and marched down to the station platform, to await the arrival of the special steam train. About two hundred of us would be packed into compartments of fifteen to twenty, some with a teacher, if we could not dodge it, but all doors were locked non-stop to Southend. Then we were let free, but all with our labels, for Southend was well used to such parties of children, most making their way to the beach or somewhat attracted to various interests along the sea-wall. A one-armed man with a sailor's cap and jacket commanding his little white terrier to run around the table to pick out a coloured silk handkerchief to our choice, then hold his hat out for a copper. An old lady invited us into her tentlike construction with a periscope; it was amusing to watch what different folk were doing in different directions of the streets outside. Then there was the boating lake, or the real little motor cars you could drive around a circuit, or a long walk out on the mud, with spade and pail to pick up live crab.

For our tea, we would all meet at James' Restaurant in the high street, for they knew just how to cope with a hungry lot of excited children. After which we would make for the kursaal with all its fun; ghost train, water-shoot and roundabouts. When all our spending money had gone, it was time to meet at the station, to be checked and rechecked until the train came in. It was more often than not that one teacher would remain behind for the next train, to bring home a child that had got lost or not realized the time.

I was about fourteen when my father was able to arrange a week's holiday for the whole family, by renting a bungalow on Canvey Island, the Leigh Bec side. My brother and I were able to ride our bikes down with my father. I remember we had to wait a while for the tide to go out, for there were no bridges. We were somewhat confined by the sea-wall, but found great enjoyment playing around in the muddy creeks. I suppose it was a holiday for my mother, she had to carry on with the meals and cook the cockles and mussels we were able to collect.

To provide extra sleeping space, for a cousin they invited down to share our great event, my father bought a hammock and we boys would take turns to sleep in the attic, which was not too successful, for the disturbance it caused when we'd fall out of 'bed' in the middle of the night on the floor above.

One afternoon my elder brother, who thought he could swim, gave us all an anxious time when he panicked and called for help when out of his depth, but help was soon offered much to our great relief. I am sure we all agreed that our seaside holiday was a real treat that few of our mates had experienced.

My father had parted with his Methodist association some years previous and had joined the parish church, of which he later became churchwarden for some twenty-five years. No difficulty arose within the family, my mother accompanied him when she could, also my sister, two younger brothers, my elder brother and myself remained Methodist. The two churches got on well together and on special occasions we would join with them at the parish church. As we got older we would be taken to Sunday evening services with my parents. One summer evening while at such a service, there was quite a disturbance to call out the voluntary firemen, who were bell-ringers and among the congregation, for they lived near the fire station close by, which housed the horse-drawn hand fire pump; a horse was always on hand, at the adjoining vicarage field.

The call was a farm fire at Eastbrookend, now the Farmhouse Tavern. What would seem very strange now, after the service had finished, the women would hurry to make tea and sandwiches to accompany their men, including the curate, and make their way across footpaths to offer all the assistance they could, to take turn on the hand-pump that resembled a ladder on each side with four men to work each side. Such was the village life in the 1920s, a real community! Everybody appeared to know one another, seldom a family moved away, or a new family moved into the village. We boys would deliver the church magazine and claim to know just who lived where. There being no local paper, folk could find out just who was born, married or died, apart from other news the vicar thought we should know.

The local doctor's wife, Mrs Prosser Evans, organised fund raising for Dr Barnado's Homes, she had a wonderful personality, it was said she had been an actress in early life. I became one of her "young helpers" and have retained the Silver Badge for my efforts. She would arrange concerts and dances, at which the doctor would auction any article that was given; he added much to the fun. Her success was largely due to her ability to meet people and talk to them while walking about the village, for very few had cars to escape in, in those days, she would almost force tickets upon you and demand you support her event. I well remember operating a side-show at her garden party, by the throwing of a tennis ball into a pail set at an angle, for a prize if it remained in.

At thirteen, I joined the Junior Guild at our church, looking back I feel it has done much to aid my self-confidence, for we were expected to speak, write a paper or even to act, always encouraged by our leaders and never ridiculed for a poor effort, of which I am in no doubt it was.

I have retained very happy memories of rambles organized by Mr Robert Lane. There would be occasions when about twenty of us would travel by train to Upminster, and then young, happy and free, we would walk across the footpaths to South Ockendon, spend a delightful time around the Hall Farm with its windmill and moat, so far-off the beaten track, then to return to the Wesleyan Chapel for a tea and evening rally. The guild included all ages of the church family, even at the social evenings. I well recall taking part in a game, where the girls were discreetly asked to put one of their shoes into a cane basket and the other one out of sight. The boy who found the right shoe would win. I had already observed the pretty new girl's footwear, which was all I needed to introduce myself, although I will confess I felt she would have been happier if it had been another boy who she knew.

By now my life will be found developing in the succeeding chapters.

SCHOOL-DAYS

My father, a local business man, having two studious children under the care of the infants' school governess, a Miss Huntley, who became personally interested in the family. I can now well imagine she, seeing what a handful I was for my mother with two younger brothers to look after, offered to relieve the situation by taking me into school a little before the prescribed age, not that this added any value to my subsequent education.

Two vivid memories remain of my infants' school. On one occasion my father appeared in the classroom at the invitation of the teacher to mend a pane of glass in the doll's house. While the rest of the children looked at me, I did not know whether to be embarrassed or feel important. The other memory was of being seated in the hall, rows of little chairs, a class to learn plain knitting with large wooden pins and a rough yarn. "In over, through off", and if it resulted in assembling enough rows of stitches and that you were lucky, she would recognise it as either a dishcloth or duster for the school ablution. I enjoyed it, for it appealed to my creative mind. Having produced what I felt, with a little consideration, could be accepted, I offered it up to my teacher, a Miss Brewster, who wore a long straight skirt, her hair swept tightly back into a bun. She viewed my efforts with her beady eyes and beamed with delight to find I had dropped a stitch several rows back. Row after row of my hard work fell from the pins until I lost heart, for I don't remember what happened to the knitting after that, except that I can still only knit plain!

The day arrived for our class to join the 'big school' only a few hundred yards along the same road, Fords Endowed School. The consoling thought at this great change was the fact that all my mates would go up with me, even if we were the little boys to meet all the big boys in the playground, for as time went on we became the big boys.

Of all trees, in that playground were two large walnut trees and a cherry, the produce of such were deemed the property of the headmaster. Often when the nuts were nearly ripe, one or two of the more venturesome boys would help themselves, and to procure the nut, one's hand would become stained peeling off the cover. This observation would fully justify the head convicting and punishing with the cane in front of the assembled school, or as happened one evening, the newly-formed school troop met and could not resist stripping the ripe cherries. I believe that warranted disbanding the school scouts for ever.

With two brothers now attending the same school I was feeling a big boy. I mustered enough confidence to set up a button pitch on the side of the playground. This required a collection of military buttons, arranged within a square area of about twelve inches, and for the payment of one trouser button or a pearly two'er the pitch owner would hand over a metal ring approx. two inches in diameter. At a given distance a boy would attempt to ring a four'er loose shank, or eight if it be a fixed shank. This would result in gaining a large bag of buttons that added something to my ego. Another playground game would be with cigarette cards. Two boys would drop a card from an agreed height, about three feet, and if it covered the previous cards you could pick all up.

As for the classes I was able to go from two to three, three to four, but then for some reason best known to the teacher, there did not appear to be room for me in standard 5, so I was stuck with the same teacher for another year, although there was little point for she had failed in the first year. I doubt if I learned much in the next year.

I was now growing up, ten to eleven years old, although the war had finished, few men had returned to work. On more than one occasion the school governor farmer arranged with our head for a class of boys to 'top' his field of beans near the school. We all agreed, an enjoyable break even if the farmer gained anything from our efforts. Before radio or television, entertainment, especially for children, was very limited. There would be some occasions we were asked to bring twopence to school when we could offer it up for an hour's travelling conjuror or Punch and Judy in the playshed after school had finished.

The post-war years created many changes at school, which was mainly staffed with women teachers. From our playground we could watch houses being built all around us — Church Elm Lane and Haresfield Road — part of the large LCC estate that brought so many new and strange children to fill our village school.

On arrival at school one morning we boys, now in the thirteen age group, were sorted out to meet a new male teacher. Being divided from the girls with a man, seemed at last we were being treated as growing up. We soon found out he was an Australian major wounded in the war and had steel plates in his head and wrist. He appeared as interested in we boys as we were in him. His eyes rested on me, "What is your name son?" he asked.

"Jack West" I answered.

"Right! I want you to take a new exercise book and write down all the boys' names in the class."

While I was carrying out his instructions, he explained to the class his method of handing out credits and debits. During the lessons I would be asked to record the boy with his due reward entered in the book. It went like this; if a boy answered a correct oral question — "credit that boy two"; if on the other hand a boy messed about he would shout "debit that boy two or three accordingly". Then on Friday afternoon I was called out to read the balance of each boy and duly hand over the book to the boy with top marks, and so it continued week after week. I never got the book again, for some reason his attitude changed towards me, and to make sure I wasn't bribing the boy with the book, on one occasion lost his temper and yelled out "debit West three dozen" — a sheer impossibility to work off.

His method of teaching was so much criticised by the other teachers who did not agree. We boys thought it strange but felt we were treated as growing up and were learning more practical things of life.

The classsroom walls were of plain green distemper. He ordered a boy to write the shipping companies and railways for large instruction coloured posters to brighten up the classroom as well as an education.

Unbeknown to us boys he accepted the *News Chronicle* challenge to write an essay on the best approach to modern teaching and won the first prize of £150. This put him further out with the head and other teachers, but with his renewed confidence he attempted many new ideas, and although I enjoyed his teaching I could never make out whether he liked me or hated me.

He apparently lodged in Hornchurch and came by steam train each day. One morning he shared his anxiety with us boys at losing his digs, and asked did any of us know anywhere he could stay? We had a large house and my parents agreed to help him for a time until he found somewhere permanent, which he accepted, with promise to my father that 'given free hand' (whatever that meant) he would make a man of me. He was keen on general knowledge and to make us more observant he would write the number of his train carriage on the blackboard and ask the boys to explain something about the figures. The boy who observed that the first three figures were the same as the last, or the whole lot added up to twenty-eight, and that was today's date, would be dished out one or two credits for such a reply.

He would stand in front of the class using his walking-stick to point or bang the desk or just hang it over his left arm. Kipling was a favourite and he loved to dramatise *On The Road To Mandalay* by using his stick for 'She would get a little banjo and play KA LA LO LO'. So much for knowledge! Teak from Burma, elephants piling it in the creeks. Other prose he rammed in us were ''Big Steamers'' telling ports of call bringing produce to England, also ''What can a little chap do''. All credit to him I can recite after sixty years.

There was one day he thought I had given him reason to keep me in class after the rest of the boys had been dismissed for lunch. He sentenced me to write a hundred lines. Taking my ruler out from my desk I duly commenced to draw the required amount. When he observed my efforts, in temper he demanded I wrote 'I must pay more attention in class'. This I did. He continued to munch his lunch while I watered at the mouth. He then dismissed me with instructions to return on time. I met my mates returning, to whom I bragged I would take my time. On returning to the class I walked across the hall and peered through the glass door fearing what kind of reception I would receive. I opened the door quietly to find my seat, to observe he was demonstrating how to light a fire in the Australian bush with a folded newspaper. The instant his eye caught me, he slung the lot at me, so I decided to give myself up to the headmaster, at least I thought he would not be in a temper. After not being surprised at anything from that class he suggested I returned home and he would put things right in the morning, and so he did, for I settled down to complete my schooling with Major Craddock.

My father had intended I should have followed my sister and brother at an advanced education, a paid school in Grays, but I made it clear it was not for me. They did not pursue the idea, but decided that I would have to stay a further year at school, for then the boys all left at fourteen years. Most parents were glad to get their boys out to work for wages.

My extra year at school gave me a little over my schoolmates. I was a big boy and often singled out for headmaster errands, out early with half-a-crown to buy 1 lb rump steak for their lunch. During this time Craddock broke the news to us boys he would be leaving us, and arranged for us to help load all his trunks into a hired van. With five or six of us he set off to find a wharf down one of the back streets of Bermondsey, where he off-loaded the cases into a rowing boat that made a couple of journeys out to a ship lying in the middle of the river. On his first return he failed to persuade me to accompany him to look over the ship. He may have had all good intentions, but the fear of setting off to sea with him was too much. As he bid us farewell he gave us a couple of coppers to refresh ourselves on the way home, and although that was the last we ever saw or heard of him he left an impression that few of us have ever forgotten.

CUBBING AND SCOUTING

The Great War had nearly finished and many of the boys of my own age had their fathers away in the services. Apart from this reason, there was an eagerness to belong to something and wear a uniform, and it was good to have a leader who could introduce us to do things for the first time other than parents, and to take us out to new places.

Now eight years old I was accepted to join my brother, a 'Sixer' under the care of Miss Auguster Earl, a Sunday school superintendent at our Methodist Church and daughter of the local builder, which gave her some added scope with contacts to keep us boys interested. We paid a subscription of ½d per week, duly marked on an official card, that I have been able to keep. We had to learn several knots and points of the compass, and were taken out for games in the spring and summer, for there were plenty of meadows available and willing farmers to co-operate.

To hold a Christmas party with little money, the Cub Mistress arranged that we all brought our own sandwiches and cakes, placed them on the table, and this would let the better off boys bring a few extras, to be grabbed up by the poorer boys, for that was the position in 1918. I do remember we all enjoyed it.

We were a good pack and most village boys of eight to eleven were proud to belong to the 1st Dagenham Wolf Cub Pack to the extent that we decided to compete in the district sports. We trained for it and got ourselves really excited for the big day. I cannot remember the exact date, but possibly the Summer of 1920, it was to be held in a meadow just before St. Laurence Church, Upminster. About fourteen of us boys were told to be at the church hall in good time to be loaded into Mr Firman's single

27

1st Dagenham Wolf Cub Pack, 1920; with Miss Auguster Earl

horse wagonette, an open carriage with a step up the back, and seated side by side facing each other. When completed the little rear door handle was turned to secure it. As full of excitement as young boys can be, we set off on the long journey down to Upminster. I well remember a pause at Eastbrookend opposite the Bell house, the horse would be led to the edge of the roadside pond to drink, and some of the boys would just cup their hands over a sunken barrel of ever running clear spring water to refresh themselves; then journeying on to reach the sports field. While we entered the various events I suppose the horse rested and nibbled the grass.

We could hardly contain our excitement on receiving the silver cup to bring home to Dagenham. The journey home seemed long and boring until we reached the village, who shared our excitement as we held the silver cup high for all to see. We wanted to fill it with lemonade on this warm summer evening, but all the shops were closed. However, we knew we could count on the generosity of the publican's wife, at the Cross Keys, Mrs Poston filled the cup with lemonade from those bottles that you had to press a glass marble down to release, and wished us well, as our excitement died away.

Some boys could never afford a uniform but they got by with the pack.

The time came all too soon to move on to the Scout Troop. This was led by Mark Sutton, a short, bearded little fellow with a keen desire to hand on to us boys much of his practical knowledge. He was a railway timekeeper, and had a son Jack in the troop. Mark Sutton looked every bit the part of the Old Wolf, and we were the Cubs or Scouts, a perfect cross-section of the village boys. On special occasions we would attend Parade Service at our Methodist Church, afterwards to be lined up outside in the street to be inspected by our District Commissioner, Mr Arthur Williams, son of Samuel Williams, Dagenham Dock.

One of our greatest delights was to be taken out for an Easter or Whitsun Monday. We would have been instructed to meet at his house in Glebe Road, for in a shed attached to the house he kept all the gear for camping. First we would draw out the trek cart and assemble the wheels to the cart, then load it with ample supplies of utensils, billycan, dixies, rope, tents etc. There could well be about twenty-five excited healthy boys all in shirts and shorts, eager to explore all the journey and a day's camp could offer, well away from the limitation of mums and dads. When all was ready to move off, two long ropes would be attached to wheel-axle pulleys and laid out in front for about twenty feet, possibly ten boys each side would take even places in order. Two older boys would be chosen to hold the handle, then the order would be given to "Pick up the rope, take the strain, quick march", and off we would wind through the streets acknowledging the cheers from our parents and friends as with great pride we set off on the great adventure.

A favourite spot was beyond Rainham, in the meadows, and splashing about in the Berwick Ponds with nothing on. Some were detailed to get the dinner ready, fry the sausages, or boil the potatoes, and if we were lucky we got plum duff for afters. At the conclusion of a very happy day we would pack it all up and return home in the same order, being greeted by various parents along the route, somewhat relieved at our safe return. We were never dismissed until back in Glebe Road with the equipment put back into the shed.

On another occasion we were all taken down to a farm at Dunton, East Hordon, for a week's camp accommodated in large bell-tents. I awoke one morning to find I had slept through what no doubt gave a few of the other boys in the tent a laugh when I discovered my legs had been blackened with my own shoe polish. I recall I did not find it as funny as they appeared to.

It was just meadows and trees to climb. In the morning two boys would be detailed to arise early to cook the large dixie of porridge and gather a pailful of mushrooms, which were plentiful in the early morning. We had two outings, one to spend our pocket-money on sweets, etc., at Pardy & Johnson General Store in Herongate, and on the Sunday we paraded for service in the red brick church up on the hill. We were able to receive letters from our mums and dads. I suppose I was about fourteen years old.

This was now the year of the 1923 World Scout Jamboree. I am not sure just where, and none of us could attend, but it was to be broadcast. This being something new and rather special, Mr Charlie Bridge had suggested to our Scoutmaster to bring us along to his hut at the rear of his little cottage near the bridge at the Church Elm. He had been experimenting with wireless, possibly one of the first in our village. We boys had hardly heard of it, never even seen one working, let alone hearing it. We all arrived very suspect and unfortunately it was very indistinct, with lots of crackle, which came from an improvised speaker in the corner of the shed. I think it was two LO calling, that part was just possible to hear. Finally we left somewhat bored, and even on the way home, questioning whether it really was reaching us the way they explained, or was someone outside the hut putting over anything that resembled the jamboree. We all found it very hard to accept.

Charlie Bridge went on to develop radio and eventually opened a sales shop in the village, to introduce many folk including our own family to this new form of entertainment. Many families brought little crystal sets with a pair of earphones they shared, and eventually end up in argument, as to the disturbance caused to find a better sport on the crystal. When valve sets with a separate speaker were introduced it was far more acceptable to the family, but required an accumulator that Mr Bridge delivered and collected weekly for recharging, until at last we were able to use the electricity supply from the mains.

It was then as a troop of robust boys, we became too much for our Methodist trustees to handle. We were offered a schoolroom by the parish church, where my father had paid twopence per week for his school, some forty years previous. What with that upheaval and the infiltration of the 'new estate' boys, plus the fact that other interests opened up. I left the troop.

WORKING AFTER SCHOOL HOURS

Jack Collard, one of my father's workmen, took a keen interest in me, and would seek every opportunity to introduce me as the governor's son. I was about fourteen years old when he told me that the man where he was working restoring a fish shop, would shortly be in need of a boy to do a couple of hours' work after school and Saturday mornings, and if I was interested he would put a word in for me. I was more than interested — I was excited with the possibility of earning five shillings per week, all of my own, for unlike most boys my parents would not expect any 'keep' from me. At my first interview I was accepted, but the next job was to sell the idea to my family. My father was not at all keen, and my brothers threatened to isolate me, as I would always smell of fish, but at least I could depend on my mother's support, for she made me the required apron of navy blue serge, tied around the waist with two tapes.

I was expected, on returning home from school at four o'clock, being sent out for some tinned fruit or something to enjoy with the bread and butter he had prepared for our tea. I was then shown the job which consisted of emptying a 1 cwt sack of potatoes into a galvanised bath on the concrete wash-down floor, and with the aid of a yard broom and plenty of water, knock them around until they were clean, lift them onto a draining board, and one by one place them onto a cutter, and with a sharp hand-pull resulted in the chips falling into a receptacle below. He would usually require about 2 cwt each night. After a time my speed increased and he would invite me into the shop and assist him with the sales, and by eight o'clock he would dismiss me with quite a liberal helping of fish and chips for my supper. On returning home my brothers would temporarily forget their resentment and willingly help me to devour my 'perks'.

This exercise continued for quite some time, until I had saved enough cash to buy a second-hand bike a 'Hobday' I remember. Telling my boss what that meant to me, he suggested I used it on Saturday mornings to ride around the new estate with a notebook and pencil to obtain orders for wet and dry fish, which I would deliver later. He fixed a large cane baker's basket with two meat hooks to the handlebars, and so I was able to increase his trade a little for which he showed his appreciation.

Not satisfied he had exploited my full sales ability, in the afternoon he had half-filled the same basket with shrimps, put in a half-pint measure, covered over with a white muslin cloth, and wished me well as I set off walking around hoping to return for more supplies. But alas, not so, for to sell shrimps in the street you had to call out "Fine Large Shrimps" or something like that in order to attract would-be buyers; I could not do that. One or two folk appeared to need them more than I cared about selling them. In despair and rather depressed I was pleased to meet a mate who, after expressing his surprise at such a task I had taken on, decided to revive my flagged spirits by eating a few of the shrimps seated under a hedge opposite the Church Elm. Disappointed with myself I returned to meet my boss and rid myself of the intolerable burden. With a sympathetic glance he lifted the cloth and exclaimed, "What have you been doing, you have not sold many!" If he did not fire me on the spot, I had already made up my mind that selling shrimps on the street was no job for me.

Not too willing to part with me, the next Saturday he asked if I would ride to Seven Kings to a friend of his and bring back a cat he intended to keep in the lock-up shop, for he had suspected mice were there. This job was far more acceptable, to have a purpose and ride out, I willingly accepted. He handed me a fish basket, the flat plaited straw type, and a wooden skewer. He showed me how to secure it once the cat was inside. I set off and found the address and was duly handed over the large tabby cat, which with some help I was able to place the skewer just as my boss had shown me, hung it over the handlebars, and set off back to the shop quite happy at my success. I had not travelled very far before the cat tried to free itself, swaying about, the lot fell off the handlebars, flip-flopping along the road, and just as I managed to grab it, it leaped out to freedom leaving me to return to the shop with the empty bag and explain just what had happened to the cat. I was somewhat relieved that my boss did not appear as upset as I had feared. I couldn't sell his shrimps and I had lost his cat, and so I decided to free myself of my first little part-time job.

Being now free in the evenings I was able to accept a job of a few hours digging over flower-beds for Curly Waits, a flower grower, for which he paid me 2/6d per evening's work. In the spring he would box up roots of pansies and daisies, load his cart and sell them to buyers at Stratford Market. Showing a keen interest in the selling he offered to take me with him. My mother woke me at 4.30 a.m. to join him at the rear of our house. The cart had been loaded the night before. It was dark but both he and the horse appeared to know the way quite well, and to stop at the Green Gate for a cup of coffee from a stall open for such early-morning callers.

Eventually we arrived at Stratford Market, I helped him unload and then took a good look round at all the other stalls. I was able to buy a large bag of cabbages for one shilling, which I brought home and was able to double my money by reselling them to friends and neighbours. It was a very enjoyable experience, although I only made the trip the once. At this stage I felt I was on course for I was earning and making money.

My mother kept a few chickens as most families did, which helped to take care to produce new-laid eggs for breakfast and a dinner now and again. It was a means of using up all the scraps from a table such as ours. Even my mother would boil potato peelings and mix some bran or 'middlings' as we call it and feed it to the hungry hens. There were times when a hen would become broody and we would be told to chase her off the nesting box, or what we preferred was to procure a dozen or so fertile eggs for her to sit on for about three weeks. Each day returning home to lunch from school we would let her out to walk around and attend to her wants, and cover the eggs with a piece of flannel. All worthwhile for the day when we came to discover first chips in the shells, and then the little balls of fluff tripping around. How proud the hen was to strut about with a complete brood of perky little chicks.

The whole idea of making some money from a simple effort within my own grasp, lead me to buy a dozen fertile duck eggs that I was able to rear and sell to the various trades people, and

c

pocket the money, my very own.

Another opportunity to earn a little cash was brought to our notice. One of my school friends was asked to gather as many boys as willing to report to Gay's Farm (now Farmhouse Tavern) to spend part of our school holiday picking up potatoes. My older brother and I duly reported with many other boys standing in the farmyard, then to be rounded up by the farm foreman and taken into the field. He had a large bundle of wooden stakes under his arm and walked up the rows placing a stake at about fifty feet intervals, and allotted the sections to two boys. We would stand within our pitch until the horse-drawn digger came along to throw out the potatoes within a three to four foot width, then with bushel boxes available, we would hasten to fill the boxes. I recall we were not the swiftest pair and the adjoining pair would be only too willing to help us clear our pitch to fill a few more boxes for their credit.

The foreman took on the role of checker, with a book and a pencil he would wander around and record each boy's amount of boxes collected. Each day we would repeat the performance to complete the field, and on Friday evening we were lined up in the farmyard to be paid by the farmer himself, Mr Ernie Gay. He checked your name and amount due at 2d per box, then would duly hand over something in the region of twelve shillings each. As we made our way home, we talked and thought of all that our cash could do for us, and decided that we were now in the position to buy our mum something; I have no idea just why we bought her a 1lb of large plums that I imagine we shared with her.

My father was always a keen gardener and did his best to encourage we boys to find some occupation within his efforts. The most outstanding thing I remember was to collect horse manure for his allotment. He had provided us with a two-wheel truck with two shafts that you could stand between as a horse, and pull around the streets, and providing some other lad had not beaten us to it, there were ample piles along the road, as it was the days of horse traffic. If we had toiled for a while without much success we knew it was always a worthwhile journey to Frizlands Lane, where a considerable amount of horse movement would leave Colsum Parrish's farmyard. Another last resort would be to drag our truck into a meadow where large piles were easily lifted, although there was a chance of being chased off for such pilfering by the farmer. When we made our report out to our father he would duly pay 2d per load. One of his allotments was on the edge of a pit and was very stony ground, so much so he would pay us 1d per tinful, to pick up stones and throw them back in the hole. We were never paid pocket-money for nothing, all had to be related to earnings.

My father had two allotments, one on the Manor Farm opposite where we lived. He always appeared very successful and produced far more than we needed. When the families moved onto the new LCC estate we kidded him on to let us get orders and deliver them in our barrows. I'm not sure who had the money, for our charges must have been low or the produce very good for we gave him worry to fulfil the orders we had taken, but it was all good fun on Friday evening to prepare it for delivery on the Saturday morning and collect the money.

We would also bunch cut flowers or spring onions and position ourselves by the roadside as factory workers left the 'Sterling' for the station, quite a good spot to sell such produce. All of which confirms the fact that our parents, by no means the poorest, were keen to encourage all of us to support ourselves, which has resulted in good training that I am sure set us on course to know the real value of money for which you had to work. This is something we are apt to forget in these more affluent times. I am sure it gave me a streak of self-confidence to go through life with.

MY FIRST JOB AND WHERE IT LED ME

I was now fifteen years old and determined to leave school and get a job, although it was not easy to make the approach. There were two main ways I discovered, first that some friend would speak up for you and tell their boss they knew of a willing lad; the second, to position oneself outside the factory gate with many others eager to offer their labour. I settled for the latter, partly to be independent. The bargain I struck with my father and the schoolmaster, was that I could go along to the Sterling Factory gate at 8.00 a.m. and if not accepted, to return to the school soon after 9.00 a.m. to continue with my lessons. This I did for a few mornings, hardly being noticed, but then came the morning I had waited for. The old man came out as usual with his list and called for cabinet-makers, tool-makers and polishers etc., for which several stepped forward, all beyond my scope. Then he looked me over, "How old are you son?" he asked.

"Fifteen sir" I replied, for I was now quite excited, but he turned to look elsewhere. This puzzled me to ask, "What do you want then?"

"A boy of fourteen" he yelled.

To which I replied, "What can a boy of fourteen do that a boy of fifteen can't?"

"It's the wages."

"How much?" I asked.

"Eleven and six, but I suppose as you are a big boy I could get twelve shillings for you."

"Right I'll take it, what is the job?"

"Helping me in the gate office."

I rushed back to school to break the news to my headmaster, hoping he would release me, plus give me a good character reference, that would not prejudice my chances, having got so far. I need not have worried, for he straight away took a piece of school notepaper, and wrote words that could not have failed me, which I have been able to keep for all these years. I am sure he was as pleased to get rid of me as I was to start my first job.

I returned back to settle down to work in the gate house, we worked like father and son; I cleaned the 'look-out' windows also the copper kettle, made tea and ran errands. After about a week he told me to write out a requisition form for pencils, pads and forms etc., take it to Mrs Taylor, and she would give me all I wanted. Not so! I had to remind her I was from the gate house, and we needed them, to which she rightly put me in my place, and reminded me she had been with the company for fourteen years and she knew how to deal with whipper-snappers like me, who just tried to grab all they could. I am sure she did much to improve my attitude toward my superiors and respect them for the position they held in the firm.

During my time at this job, the General Strike of 1926 greatly affected the factory. Although I was considered staff and loyally reported each day, I was used to help load our lorries with supplies for London, all behind solid iron gates, then to look out in the road for a petrol lorry convoy that our lorries may join in with. Another incident I recall was for me to find a Mr Whatley working in the factory, to pass on a message we had received for him to return home at once, as his little boy had been burned with others in a shed packed with bonfire rubbish for Guy Fawkes' night. This was a fatal tragedy, and the 'new estate folk' extended their real sympathy to the 'villagers'.

I had now come to the point of dealing with my wages. My mother suggested I gave her five shillings a week for my keep, and that she would look after a further five shillings, that I would need for clothes. This left me with one shilling and sixpence, apart from tips I would pick up. I also had a few War Saving Certificates, that my father had purchased for us, when a real field gun was placed outside the parish church during the First World War, to encourage folk to save. They would stamp them with a gun impression.

It was about the time I started work that our farmer friends sold their Manor Farm opposite where we lived, to an estate agent who planned roads and building plots, to sell to anyone who wished to avail them. My father and his brother, having lost their allotments through the change, decided to purchase a plot each for £60 freehold. As this was considered difficult for some folk, the agents arranged a quarterly payment sum for a few years, and then finally receive the deeds. I worked out that all I needed was six pounds' deposit, and for five years, two pounds fourteen shillings every quarter, and then receive the freehold deed when I was twenty-one. At sixteen years old I walked into the estate agent's office on a Saturday afternoon, where he showed me the plan of Aldborough Road, they had no more available near my father's plot. Somewhat disappointed, I went to tell my father, who was digging and chatting to my uncle on the next plot. I told him how upset I was, and that I had been offered an irregular plot near the footpath, for ninety pounds. My uncle suggested I take over his plot and he would accept the larger one, and subsequently my father built a bungalow for the family. I gained for he had partly dug the newly acquired plot I owned. Now I could grow vegetables to sell, and gain some extra money toward the repayment.

The roadways remained grass tracks for many years. I was given an old wooden shed that I erected near the road, this brought me in a further five shillings a week, to garage a fellow's car. After a time, water and electricity services were laid if we needed them. I duly visited the agent's with my little black receipt book, bearing a twopenny stamp each payment, this I have kept as a reminder. During this time I had visited my uncle's garden at Stifford and admired a long row of sweet peas just bursting into bloom, he offered me the row for five shillings. Several mornings afterwards I arose at six o'clock to cycle down and pick several bunches and return back at nine o'clock to my office job, where they were eagerly snapped up for one shilling and sixpence per bunch.

After one year as 'gate boy' I was promoted to the cost office with a rise to sixteen shillings per week, but it was a job I became thoroughly bored with, adding up figures all day. I hardly need have told my boss how I felt, for I am sure he had not considered I was much help to him. I asked if I could be transferred to the woodwork shop, which was making solid mahogany radio and switchboard cabinets, this appealed to me, but no, they transferred me to the radio testing dept. There I assisted with the inspection and testing, polishing sets to perfection, for London exhibitions. Then instructed to carry them through to the packing department, one placed above the other, carried with great care, I set off, and all would have been well if some idiot had not left a trolley in my pathway, which caused me to stumble over and drop the sets on to the concrete floor. Not knowing whether to bunk off home, or return to face it! I decided to be a man and face all I deserved, but the tester just told me it was a pity, and we would have to prepare two more.

I could not settle down after that, and again had another attempt to go into the woodwork shop, for I had heard it was possible to earn a bonus for extra effort. I was finally accepted to join them. There were many more boys my age as well as experienced cabinet-makers. We boys were formed into a gang, a poor lot, mainly from East Ham and Barking. One boy would assemble the dovetail joints loosely, I would hold them under a tap of boiling glue, another would place them in a clamp, another clean them off, and pack them ready to be finished off on a revolving sander belt. "Sweat in" was the cry for speed. Our intense work was broken mid-morning and afternoon, by what we felt was a most attractive young girl with the tea-trolley. The boys were often skint and would borrow from me, to be duly repaid when wages arrived on Friday. I was a sort of banker for them for I was never short of money, but the poor kids had fares to pay, and the support for their keep never left them much to spare.

It was when I realised, with all my effort I was only getting nineteen shillings a week, that I suggested to my father I felt I could do the same work he was paying his men at three pounds per week, and so he agreed to give me a chance to prove myself. A carpenter's apron was found for me and I started by punching nails and puttying up upon a greenhouse we were providing for one of our Harrow Drive clients. From this I naturally followed my brother, coffin-making from solid timber. By now my weekly wage was averaging two pounds per week from which I was saving a surplus.

Unbeknown to the rest of my family, I showed sufficient interest in a motor cycle for Harry Allerton to tell me he knew of a little Royal Enfield two-stroke, hardly used, the old man had paid twenty-five pounds for it, but was willing to accept fifteen pounds. I was keen, so the next Thursday afternoon he closed his shop and drove me down in his 1926 Bull-Nosed Morris Cowley Tourer (that he had taught me to drive) to a little red brick cottage by the bridge in Nag's Head Lane, Brentwood. He introduced me to a country-looking fellow, possibly in his fifties. He opened the door of the shed that revealed the motor cycle in brand-new condition. It appeared he had spent more time cleaning it, than riding it. Harry started it, and showed me the controls, I had often watched other boys, but never ridden myself, now I was being offered the chance of my life.

With fifteen pounds in my pocket, I rode up the lane. It was quiet, no other traffic about, I felt like a bird with wings. On and on until I remembered to return and assure them all was well. I could ride, and I could pay for it. I collected my receipt and decided to return home via Navestock and show my friends at the farm all I had acquired that afternoon. I did not do so well to enter my village, I had used up all the petrol. I had arranged with Harry to hide the bike in his shed, from my family. After a few days my father discovered my means of rapid mobility. "You had better let me have the particulars of that bike for insurance, I do not want to be responsible for your misdeeds." I considered he had accepted it.

It did give me a wider range to enjoy my spare time, for on one occasion I rode to Yarmouth in the rain, without any special clothing, to meet my mate who was staying at his aunt's. Arriving soaking wet and not being offered any 'drying out', I settled for the cinema, which was warm and comfortable.

By now feeling more responsible and independent I began to feel life offered many opportunities. Around this time my elder brother had bought an old two-seater car from a man in the village. It was a 1914 Humber, resembling an armchair on wheels, with brass lamps and a hood that strapped on if it should rain. To own a car in those days was an achievement, for you had to be keen to take it to pieces and put it together

again, hoping it would run better. My brother fell well within
that class. One never spent time learning to drive, you just
learned the controls, and providing you could miss the few farm
carts, you were accepted on the road. Almost as soon as he
found out how it worked, my father had an urgent call to
arrange a funeral at an address in Upminster. They both set
off, and to our great relief, returned mission accomplished.
When more spares were required they settled to buy a similar
model and make a good car from the two, the latter had an
open sports body with a little more appeal. On one occasion he
made a bargain with me, if I helped him pack up some kit,
while he completed a repair on it, we could venture to the Isle
of Wight where our two younger brothers were in camp with
the Scouts. The repair took a long time, but eventually we left
about four o'clock in the afternoon; he was about eighteen and
I seventeen.

Welded together with exciting adventure, Barking, East
Ham, Woolwich Ferry, Lewisham, Lee Green, and at
Kidbrook Common the car packed up, and so we decided to
camp with our tent on the common and do the repair in the
morning. We slept well, only to be woken up by some old
farmer out shooting rabbits, grumbling that we had no right on
his ground. He stood over us while we put all our gear in the
car and pushed it to an adjoining air force station, and were
well received, even given some breakfast.

With the repair completed we journeyed on, hopefully.
About midday we stopped beside the road to cook some chops
that had become a little stale, and it was while we were eating,
that a man showed an interest in us. When we told him that
we'd had trouble with our car and that nobody wanted us, he
assured us that we would be welcome to spend the night on the
farm where he boarded, not far along the road. Sure enough
when we got going he was leaning over the field gate to
welcome and show us the best place to pitch our tent, at the top
of the hill, in case of rain. We could collect milk and eggs at the
farm. It was a lovely evening to enjoy a cooked meal outside
and settled for the night. But alas we were awoken early in the
morning, this time with water dripping through the tent. It was
Bank Holiday Monday and it rained the whole day. Apart from
nipping out for milk etc., we were confined to the tent all day.

Dejected and homesick I persuaded my brother to give up the venture and return home, even if the sun shone all next day, and it did. I am sure he was disappointed with me, for he set off the next day on his own to some place in Suffolk, only to return with a summons, for passing a patrol policeman on the wrong side. He continued with his car while I enjoyed my motor bike.

When I became eighteen years old, still only a boy in my father's eyes, he condescended to let me attend a funeral with him. It was an old man of the village, and very heavy to be carried upon the shoulders of four part-time coffin bearers to the churchyard. I was to act as a reserve if needed, and this required me to dress in funeral attire. Using my father as a model, I gathered some of his left-offs, but found great difficulty in fixing the stiff collar, all so strange to a teenager's idea of dress. I found the best fitting top hat and frock-coat. After one look in the mirror I intended to give the whole idea up, I was certain everybody would stand and stare at me.

My mother did her best to minimise my embarrassment, ''your father is depending on you'', (which I doubted) and so with all the courage I could muster I settled upon a route that would get me to the point of pick-up, by all the back ways I knew, where I found the rest of the men dressed the same. It all passed off without much notice of me and I duly received the wage of six shillings for about two hours. This accelerated my interest in funerals. As fate would have it, the very next funeral was only a few houses away from where we lived. I only needed to walk out to join the rest, when I heard one of the children call out ''Mum, come and see Jack West he's got a funeral hat on''; another hurdle over. By this time I felt well initiated into the funeral trade.

During my late teens, I developed a strong relationship with the Navestock Farm boys, which became a real outlet from the New Dagenham that had taken over so many farms, to provide the huge housing estate. Also, I suppose working for my father, sometimes funeral, sometimes building work, I could relieve my frustration for there would be less funerals in the summer. My father detected, that all I wanted was the funeral side, I was not lazy, but always hoped I could absorb my full time on that side of our firm, and that one day we would own our carriages instead of having to hire each time.

Although my father was a builder at heart, and had served a rigid apprenticeship, he was more keen to progress than his partner, who possessed no desire to depart from building work, or expand in any way, for my father often had to slow us boys down; to be fair to his partnership Mr Coe never experienced the responsibility of a family, which I suppose he regretted, for I doubt it was by choice. My father did try to satisfy both sides, for after a lot of persuasion they both agreed we took over a shop, at Lodge Avenue, as a branch. On 17th October 1934 we signed the lease for twenty-one years. My father knew the owner, who promised we could drop out after three years if we found it too hard going. Looking back I am sure they both felt at least it would get me off their backs, and I suppose it did for it was hard going, mostly young people and a strong pull to return back to their Cockney undertakers. Also the Co-op had a very strong pull, with their dividend, and so what orders we did receive we worked hard to compete with a good service.

Staffing a lock-up shop was difficult at times, shop hours were nine to six and nine to nine on Saturdays, our average of two funerals per week was hardly enough, and so we made up the time by taking over all the work from the main shop. This enabled me to take on a boy to help with the work and to look after the shop should I have to leave for any reason.

During the years 1930-39 which seemed to me so full of opportunities, although it started with a depression, we worked hard and enjoyed the simple things of entertainment. In June 1931 my only sister was married at Dagenham Parish Church. With four teenage brothers to help, it all went with a swing, and the village was made well aware of it. My father had a marquee erected at the White House, in the garden. It was a wet day, and we almost forgot to collect the ice-cream we had ordered.

By now I had paid for my ground, for I was twenty-one, and received the title deeds. Little self-built bungalows were sprouting up, which tempted me with the idea; I put to my brothers (also working in the firm on the building side) that we might attempt to build a bungalow to make some money for ourselves, as our firm never seemed to engage on house building at that time. After agreeing to co-operate, he drew the

plans and deposited them, with the Urban District Council of
Dagenham. When they were accepted we started work, with
one aim in mind, to keep the cost to the minimum. We were
able to find sand and ballast in the plot without digging too
deep. This work, with digging out the foundations, and a few
pounds to buy some cement, we were able to make a good start.
Next were bricks, and it so happened that while talking to our
local estate agent, he offered me a row of four cottages he had
received orders to demolish. For the cost of £10 I could have all
the bricks. His men threw the bricks anywhere, my job was to
find a couple of boys to clean off the mortar, then have a horse
and van to transport them to the site. All went well, my brother
was able to build the walls up to about three feet so that we
could walk round to see just where the rooms were. All seemed
to be going well, until one day while riding his motor bike up
the yard, his clutch cable broke, resulting in him breaking his
ankle as he crashed into the shop opposite. All work stopped for
about two months. A little frustrated we got into gear again to
complete the brickwork, and make every effort to get the roof
on before the winter. Now looking nearly completed from the
outside, the interior seemed an endless job, although we
engaged a contractor to plaster the walls, which made a rapid
transformation both inside and out.

Springtime came and we had a surplus of energy, for we
would get up at six-thirty in the morning, over to Valence
Open Air Baths for a quick dip, then return to spend an hour
on the bungalow, then at nine o'clock begin work with our
firm. We were both very fit and willing to expend all our time
for the due reward later.

By now we had got to the stage where we felt it would be
better if we could borrow a little money to complete, for
although we had done quite well, such things as bath and basin,
fireplace and fittings would cost quite a lot. My mother
suggested we approach Miss Wright, better known to the
family as Aunty Bessie, for she was always keen to encourage
those that tried to help themselves. My mother had kept up
quite a good relationship since leaving her domestic situation
with the family, for many years, prior to her marriage. Either
she or I made the appointment at her home, next to
Hornchurch Church, a lovely house my firm had built for them

some years previously. I was received by the maid, who after consulting her mistress, invited me into the drawing-room to sit down and expound all my hopes of how to work hard and get rich. All of which I was assured, was music to her ears, for she appeared so interested, to the extent she asked, "How much do you think you need?" Feeling by now she was keen to have a part in the venture, I asked for one hundred pounds, to which she got up from her chair, walked over to the small bureau in the corner, for me to observe her write a cheque. As she handed it to me, she spoke some of the wisest words that I have since repeated to folk who have approached me in later years, "Here you are Jack, here's fifty pounds — you see if you can finish with this, you will only have to repay me fifty pounds instead of one hundred, but don't hesitate to return if you really need more. How much do you intend to sell it for when it's completed?" I guessed at a figure of five hundred and fifty pounds, as that was about the going price and there were plenty for sale. I thought no more of that until she told me later that it was her intention to buy it for my aunt, who had also spent time in service with her family, and that she could repay how and when she could. This immediately took a load off our minds, and gave us great incentive to complete, ready for my aunt to move in. When the cheque came to share with my brother, sure enough we had only the fifty pounds deducted. I walked about with the largest bank balance ever I had expected.

During the building period I had enjoyed my motor bike, but now the way had opened up to own my own car, for my father had never driven, and we had no modern family car. Although I had borrowed one at times, holding a licence since becoming eighteen (that I have still kept). After searching through various adverts I finally bought a four door, coach built Morris Cowley Saloon 1931 model, MU 2504, for fifty pounds, it was in very good condition, from a sale yard, Acre Lane, Brixton. I drove it home and parked it in our front garden overnight. Although I went to sleep, to wake up and find I had not been dreaming for there was sure enough my very own first car. Now quite proud to take my mother and father out in it for rides, which were a treat in itself, in those times.

I was now even more popular than ever with the fellows and girls at our church club, that on walking home one evening, we decided to try and arrange a caravan holiday. We contacted a man at Cheshunt, who had advertised his five-berth caravan for hire, and after fitting a tow bar, and mustering enough courage, I was able to tow it back to our yard, all through the built-up area. This gave me the confidence to attempt a tour to Devon, with Ern Green as navigator, his sister Lil as cook, Arthur and Linda to look after each other. I joined the AA for some support if we should need it. We packed our supplies and equipment the night before, and after a family farewell and their good wishes for our great adventure, we set off on our planned route. However, we did have reason to call upon the AA as the clutch was not at all happy with such weight to pull up the hills, even though they all got out and walked up, and it may be hard to believe in these times, but I got out myself and held the accelerator down, as I walked beside. Why we chose Devon I was never sure, but such lovely rides through north to south following the Exe River as it wound its way through such lush pastures, and to walk across the downs at Torquay, to suddenly view Anteys Cove from above, in brilliant sunshine, with so many young people swimming out to the raft. We were young, 'we were free', to join in all that came our way.

One midday we stayed for lunch at a very pretty little village called Bickley. While there, we were approached by an old farmer, who was disappointed we had to decline his invitation to spend a night on his farm. These were days when cars and more so caravans were few to tour Devon, for village folk welcomed us, even for a chat. After two weeks we all returned home, well tanned and happy, and so to work.

In Dagenham many young families were feeling the strain of the Depression, money was scarce and with its large proportion of young children, scarlet fever and diphtheria were very common complaints; sadly we buried many, which put added burden upon the poorer families, for they had let their insurance go. What with rail fare and rents, wages that seldom exceeded £4 per week, debt was piling up all round. Housewives would flip from one baker or milkman to another, in order to find fresh credit. We as a firm were losing nearly as much as we were making. I suggested to my father that I should visit those responsible and discuss the possibility of collecting two or three shillings per week, for at least this would bring some money in, and after a while, wipe the slate to retain good relations for better times. It worked in most cases. On a Saturday morning I would ride round on my motor bike to collect from houses, the children would call, "Mum, it's the undertaker", week after week it became a friendly call, as they co-operated we took the opportunity to show mercy and did 'wipe the slate clean' and so retain the firm's good relations with the families. However there was one woman who asked to be left for a few weeks, and on receipt of her Christmas Loan Club payout, she would settle up. When I did call the house was empty. I went straight round to the rent office for a forwarding address, only to be met with, "if we knew we wouldn't tell you, for we want all she's got". Yet the whole venture was well worthwhile. Apart from the money received, I lived to have the opportunity to meet the grown-up children to arrange their parents' funerals. By then I had learned to respect these women for the way they managed to bring up a family on such low income, no DHSS, no Family Allowance or Welfare Benefit, and yet those children affectionately required the best for their mums and dads.

Times changed, the years just prior to the war were happy times, never believing war would be possible, but September 1939 life abruptly changed; never to be the same again.

ROMANTIC YEARS

Compared with today's ratings, I suppose I would be considered a slow starter, and this could well be due to the fact that I was very happy and carefree within my own family, with three brothers and a sister, of whom I failed to understand just why other fellows found her so much more attractive than I did.

My earliest admiration for a girl of my own age, was to be found with Freda, a chubby auburn-haired girl of fifteen, whose pleated school uniform failed to conceal her attractive figure. My young eyes would have loved to explore, but for the fear that she might tell her mother, who was responsible for my mother's weekly wash. Any meetings with Freda were at my home. She sometimes helped me to gather and sell the produce from my plot. I am sure we were too shy to make any further advances, and so the relationship just petered out.

With others parents, my father was responsible for organising dances for the young people at the church hall, having I suppose, vested interest, with five teenage children himself. We all attended with added confidence. I recall an occasion; one evening, the dance had finished, when the boys would return to their side in a click; as the girls returned to leave the dance floor free, I noticed the ribbon fall from the plaits of a very dignified young girl, and lay in the middle of the dance floor. Almost spontaneously I caused 'catcalls' from my boys, as I walked across, picked up the ribbon and returned it to the owner. I considered it all worthwhile, as her father was an army captain. I continued a friendly association, but as she attended boarding-school, it soon faded out.

My next experience was when at seventeen, my father sent

me to a local engineering factory, to paint a large machine assembled in their yard. After a day's intensive work, I left the yard along with the rest of the staff, and was surprised to find I was the point of interest with a very pretty young girl, waiting by the gate beside her cycle. She offered me an inviting smile, that intrigued me to respond, which found us most awkwardly riding side by side, when she was able to tell me that she had observed me during my working day and would only be happy to spend a time with me. Enjoying such attention, I found I had accompanied her nearly home to Goodmayes.

She explained any nearer her home might prove embarrassing for her, and so we arranged to meet the following Saturday afternoon. It never left my mind until we met at the arranged point. She informed me, she would first have to call upon her girl-friend, to tell her she was supposed to be with her if her mother should ask, "so don't go round to my mother asking for me." Having sealed all leaks, we rode around just happy to be with each other. During our conversation I discovered that she knew more about me than I had realized, from one of our club girls that worked in the same office. She had tried to help by inviting her to our Club Social Evening, that did it! for I never intended bringing this girl within focus of my club members, far less accompanying her back home late at night. Therefore I made it quite clear, she could go if she wished, but I was not going if she did! Which resulted in another fade out.

For the next two or three years, I spent holidays with my friends from Navestock Farm. They had an aunt living near Yarmouth, where they were able to stay for a couple of weeks. I found a bed and breakfast room in North Quay, Yarmouth; it was about the limit of my funds. I recall a photo of her three handsome daughters on the piano, one of which I longed to have met, but apparently, mother was not so keen. The old lady would cook a good breakfast, egg and bacon and always put a cottage loaf with plenty of butter and marmalade. She must have felt I was hungry, for I would cut a couple of large slices for our lunch after a swim, then for fish and chips (1/6d) late in the afternoon. Yarmouth had much to offer the teenagers, with its two piers and exciting fun-fair, that gave us ample opportunity to chat up other girls on holiday, to end up with a walk along the beach in the moonlight. The *'Daily*

Mirror Eight' troop of girls that would display all that young boys' eyes could feast on. Also to add to the revelry, were the Scottish girls that spent the season working on the herring trade. Yarmouth never failed to excite the young folk.

I continued free and unattached. As I passed my twenty-first birthday, I found myself attracted to a smart good-looking girl who would pass our house each evening, home from work. I was able to find the courage to walk beside her and have a chat, for which I had to withstand the rebuff "I don't even know you", whether that was entirely true, I wasn't too sure, but all too soon she stopped to indicate we were very near her home.

Quite a happy association continued, but strangely I was never invited in, which resulted in some quite long waits outside her house in my car, the price I paid to get right away and be alone with Nina. This continued until one evening, after waiting a little too long, I developed a mood that made me wonder whether it was all worthwhile. This evening we journeyed out to Brentwood without hardly speaking a word to each other, until while climbing a hill at Warley I realized a tyre was flat. A dirty, wet, dark night, half-way up a hill to jack a car up was an occasion where I was willing to accept all the help and sympathy that Nina was more that willing to offer me. A few summer months passed with a friendship I was finding hard to develop or even continue, and so I decided to explain this in clear terms. On returning back one evening, being quite late, I had hoped to make a quick and simple termination, but not so, for she refused to leave the car unless I promised to meet her the following evening. Twelve o'clock passed, one o'clock! until I suggested leaving the car and walking home, and collecting it in the morning, but eventually she accepted my intention. Another girl to gradually fade out of my life. Feeling free again I had no difficulty to rejoin my friends, especially a fellow who never appeared interested to stray as I did.

As time passed I realized how my work brought me in contact with some quite nice girls in a non-commital sort of way. I had developed a floral wreath agency with Madame Olga, who also managed a dancing school, of which the girls would assist with the floral wreath making. Should it be that I needed assistance to deliver large family orders, Olga would whisper "take your pick", and I knew the girl that enjoyed an ice-cream and a little ride out to be alone for a while together, but nothing more.

I was never quite sure why I should have attracted girls so easily, for the sweet-shop girls opposite our Lodge Avenue branch, would go to any lengths to command my attention. I would go out to my car on leaving to lift a note from under the wiper, and read all the nice things I would never give them the opportunity to tell me. On another occasion my father passed on an address in the Lodge Avenue area that I was to return to, to arrange a funeral, only to be met by one of the sweet-shop girls, who hastened to hold the front door behind her and foolishly explain there was no business to attend to, but pleaded for forgiveness, for she just had to talk to me, poor kid. On another occasion I answered the phone to hear a girl tell me how she had seen me conducting a funeral through the street (top hat and tails), that I had so infatuated her she just had to speak with me, but refused to identify herself.

I am sure I entered into a life of romance, for romance sake, spurred on by conceit that was thrust upon me. I was free, and intended to remain free, for there was always something or somebody better, and more exciting. Although I had to stand such remarks from mothers, who would say "how many more girls' hearts are you going to break?" I continued on, even with imagination. On one occasion, seeing a pile of five-bar field gates at the sawmills, I longed to put into practice my romantic idea to track around the farms, to sell gates with the hope I might meet a wealthy farmer's daughter; alas! I never put the idea into practice.

Of course there were periods when my work would absorb me. As one day a lady walked into my offices to arrange her mother's funeral, who had died above the next shop flat. I apologized for not even knowing anyone was even ill so near. I prepared a nice coffin which was to remain in the lounge, explaining that I would return later to fix the engraved inscription plate on the lid. This I did, afterwards to be invited into the living-room to confirm the arrangements, where my eyes fell upon what I felt was the most beautiful girl I had ever seen. She was arranging her birthday cards, all so out of context with the sombre business that I was there for. The cards told me that she was eighteen years old. I tried my best to dismiss the effect it had upon me, feeling quite sure she would never be interested in me, or my admiration for her; even apart from the fact I would be expected to keep my place and act professionally. Having completed all that I had been engaged for, it was no easy job to forget Joyce, and to my sheer delight, a few days later, she entered my office with a message from her mother, and surprised me with the interest she showed in my work. She told me of her typing ability in a local office, if ever I needed any help. By the weekend I had arranged for a little typing I needed, but what was more I laid on a little tea, for just us two, that we both enjoyed. I also arranged, that we should drive out the following Saturday away from the work, to be alone in the country, to learn more of each other's hopes and dreams, and so the friendship continued. I felt so proud, I wanted to take her everywhere with me, thinking others would love and admire her as much as I did.

A Sunday came, when it was arranged for Joyce to meet my family for tea, my two brothers' girls would be interested, I was assured. I called for her at the appointed time, only to find she had tightly permed her lovely fair hair, that I had been allowed to brush. She looked so sophisticated. I think I must have shown my disappointment, for she reluctantly brushed it out. Not a good start, but we got through the family reception quite well, or so I thought, until she told me afterwards that she did not think she had been received as well as she had expected. I did fear my family felt that she was not quite the girl they had in mind for me. Her confidence was equal to my own, for she ran a dance school. I arranged a visit to the Palladium to see a pantomime, that was a very happy occasion. My grandmother and aunt had hoped that I would drive them down to visit a friend for the day at the lovely village of Bennenden. Their willingness to accept that Joyce could accompany them made it a very happy day, spent in a little thatched cottage with an open wood fire. It was Easter and the lanes were carpeted with primroses. We were both caught up with admiration for each other and everything around us. A day that was perfect in tune.

There were times when Joyce would call in on returning home from work, to watch me polish a coffin, her immaculate dress and sheer beauty would so frustrate me, that with my hands soaked in French polish I had to ask her to leave, for I could not respond without clean hands. One day she gave me a coloured portrait that she'd had taken especially for me, and I would gaze upon it before going to sleep. I so admired her, and the fact that she thought so much of me, I was sure other boys were envious. Her mother had booked a holiday at Southend and we arranged to drive her mother and little brother and sister down on a Saturday afternoon, being well compensated by the drive home together. She had prepared herself to sleep alone in the flat; on return we unlocked the door and I accompanied her to the beautifully furnished lounge, graced by the vase of pink roses I had given her the night before, which did their best to tell her that I loved her. The whole setting was heaven itself. We spent a while trying to take in all it meant to be there alone together. Then determined not to spoil it in any way I bid her good-night as I had usually done.

During the next week, we again arranged to visit Southend and try and meet the family. Our evening was somewhat spoilt, for it took us so long to find them. The ride home was not quite the same, for she told me that one of the shop girls had been staying with her at nights and that she was eager not to be too late. Before she put the key in the door, she bluntly told me, "You don't really love me". This astounded me to reflect that her jealous girl-friend had prompted her to challenge me. Before I offered any defence I realized she was right! I had no idea of contemplating marriage, just enjoying romance for romance sake, but to be dropped was too great a blow to my pride. In my own heart I knew if only I could regain her affection and that I could be the one to terminate, I would restore my pride. The more I tried the more I felt the loss. I tried to get over it, I bought a new car and regained my boy-friend's companionship who suggested we spent an exciting weekend in Paris.

As life became full again, another girl faded out of my life. My friend also arranged that we spent a holiday in the Lake District at a Methodist Guild Holiday Home. When we arrived, we found that all the young folk were boarded in the annexe to sleep, while the older respectable sedate folk slept in the big house. Within the grounds there were various animals kept, which tempted the young folk to get hold of a few ducks to let loose in the dormitories. On another occasion we got the

Myself 24 years

donkey out on the front lawn at midnight, only to receive threats of being sent home in the morning for causing a disturbance to the guests. I feel we righted ourselves when spending days climbing Helvellyn and Langdale Pikes, to return for a shower and a good evening meal followed by an impromptu concert.

The next summer we decided to tour Devon, just Ern and I, with a tent, determined to accept anything that came our way, youth hostel, farmhouse, or just our tent. We really did enjoy the lanes and the remote little villages, for there were few cars down there in those days, that folk were still pleased to chat with us. After a day's touring around we would try and find a night's accommodation. When we enquired of an 'old yokel' he directed us well off the beaten track, to a farm where we might expect to stay for the night. Driving into the farmyard, we were met by what turned out to be the farmer's daughter, who replied, "No, we don't, although I believe the people here before us did." (Our car was nice, and we were both about her age.) "Wait a while, I'll see Mother." A few moments later she returned to say we could stay, just for the night.

We followed her into the farmhouse, we were offered some supper and shown our room. After a lot of speculation we settled down to sleep. In the morning we were woken by Mary, handing us a silver tray with morning tea in fine china. Such a quality of kindness was a little overwhelming. We washed and dressed and were shown the breakfast room with ample home-made butter and clotted cream. I became somewhat intrigued by the display of silver cups and plates, of which the inscription revealed we were now staying on a stock breeding farm of some standing within the county. Mary entered to say, "I suppose you realize why we do not accept just anybody to stay here."

By now I contended we were being quite well accepted, for Mary asked what our intentions were for the day. On the beach at Torquay only a few miles away, for it was a grand day, all we did was swim and sunbathe. With my eyes closed I could imagine all sorts of things about Mary and the farm. Before we left, Mary assured us her mother had said we could stay another night, if we wished. Toward late afternoon I reminded my friend, who agreed we should return to the farm, where we found a real welcome from Mary, who asked if we had done any shooting, for she was willing for us to accompany her. With all the bluff I could muster, I said I had a little experience, and was willing to come, to which she handed me a loaded gun. As we set off across the meadows, reminding me to be careful over the stiles with the gun, Mary seemed very confident and made two or three shots, resulting in a couple of rabbits, which I offered to carry, until she realized 'poor old Jack had not had a shot yet'. Assuring me that when we passed through the next hedge, there were usually a few shots at the top of the meadow, and sure enough there was. I lifted my gun and took aim, trying my best to at least look the part. Mary also lifted her gun, and the second she fired I followed 'bang bang', and sure enough when we went along to the spot, a rabbit lay ready to pick up. I'll never know just whether it was the result of my effort or Mary's, although she gave me all the credit. Home we journeyed to place the rabbits in the dairy. By now we had conversed enough to have developed a mild friendship, of which my mate appeared quite satisfied with the by-products that were being offered.

Father Wills in a little more detached mood, asked if we strong lads would care to give him a hand to bring a few young pedigree bulls down from the hills, to tether them to a stake in the yard, to tame them a little before the sale. Anything to show off our strength and fitness was acceptable. As we journeyed up the hill, Father explained, to hold the bull one had to pull the rope sideways, which I did my best until it ran faster than I could, but somehow all turned out well, for it found itself tied to the stake in the yard, for us to drive around to obtain the desired state.

The next day we decided to leave the farm and journey on to explore more of the little villages. Toward evening we had strayed well out to find somewhere for the night. A signpost directed us to Little Hempstead. The road narrowed over a stone bridge which led up to a church. When it came to what appeared an abrupt end, we stopped to find where we were being led, when from outside a quaint little inn, a girl's voice enquired, "Are you lost?" One look at this girl, of about our own age, I asked if she knew where we could stay for the night. Her reply was that they did bed and breakfast but they were full up, but wait, when she soon returned to say her daddy had offered a tent on the lawn, if that would suffice. Another look at this open-hearted natural girl, I would have been prepared to have slept in the coal cellar, to have received any attention from her. As we followed to inspect the tent on the lawn, she hastened to bring out extra pillows and offer some supper of cold rabbit pie or pigs' kidneys, with a drink of their home-made cider. We settled down to sleep, but for myself a little restless until she welcomed us with a real good egg and bacon breakfast. We must have left a good impression for they only charged us two shillings and sixpence with the offer to return for another night if we wished. As for myself, I would have loved to have received more of her hospitality and almost affection, offered by one so desiring friendship from boys of her own age.

We spent the next day around Bovey Tracey, including some fishing, we could see the fish swimming up and down, but could not catch any. In a very secluded stream on this warm summer's day, a kingfisher more gifted than we continued to swoop up and down the stream. We enjoyed the day, and all we saw and did, to be reminded it was nearing time to find another night's accommodation. I noted a signpost to Little Hempstead; somewhat hesitating, I reminded my mate the girl had offered us if we wished to return, and it was only two shillings and sixpence. He agreed so we were welcomed back for another night.

On returning home I wrote to both girls, to tell them just how much they had added to our holiday spent touring Devon. At the following Easter, my suggestion of spending a long weekend with Mary on the farm was willingly accepted. By now, we felt much more at home, both with Mary and the farm, and were quite eager to split a pile of sawn logs, of which Mary took a snap. Still concerned we were enjoying ourselves, she offered us the guns, to at least frighten the pigeons, if not shoot them as they were a real menace. And so we were able to keep up a valuable platonic friendship by writing to each other.

By 1941 my father had found his work had greatly impaired his health. I was now away at Aldershot, and hoped that Mary would be able to give my mother and father a holiday, being provided with the dairy produce that could make a rationed diet not too difficult. They enjoyed their stay and I wrote to thank Mary for all she had done for my parents. After that our future friendship was lost in the mists of a prolonged war and my overseas service.

At the beginning of the war I had continued to work, and bought a new bicycle, I was reminded it was a good investment, more so as petrol would be rationed. It was an odd time to live through, folk were much more friendly, there was always an easy topic of conversation. Girls seemed more plentiful, as many fellows of my age, or a little younger, were away in the forces. I recall being very attracted to what I considered a fine healthy girl, for as she made her daily journey on her sports cycle to a local office, her fair hair blowing in the wind, her brown coat and yellow scarf so attracted me, for me to decide one evening to make the same journey on my cycle, and to chat with her as we rode side by side. I suppose it was her happy reaction that pleased me, but when she asked where I lived, I had to confess not in her direction, but I just liked riding to accompany her. We parted and arranged to meet again, which we did, and Florie accepted an invitation for a drive out to South Weald on the following Sunday. Life seemed brighter for both of us, we longed to be alone together and find out more about each other.

The time came when Florie had to admit she had a boy-friend away in the forces, and that on his next leave he intended to seek her engagement. She assured me she liked me quite a lot and was most happy to spend time with me. Her lovely natural disposition confessed how torn she was, in fear she would be bound to upset one of us and she was not certain just who it should be. It dawned on me that I might be stealing his girl while he was away on active service. I was, I am well sure, compensated as I then tried to act her brother, to make up her mind for her, for I had no plans to seek her engagement. It was an experience I would not have missed for I was assured it was for the right cause, when she was able to put down on paper all that she felt and appreciated. 'A beautiful ship to pass in the night.'

I remained very popular among the club girls. Some evenings to load my car with four or five all unattached, all would, I am sure, have been willing to be the last one dropped off, but that was my decision, and so I would plan a route to where I would receive my special good-night kiss. It was during 1939 that the council had built a brick air raid shelter at the rear of our club hall, and during an evening one girl kidded me on to show her just what we would have to do in the event of a raid during a club night. Eager to explore the building myself, we left the hall to enter and look around in semi-darkness, for there were no windows. While we were discovering alone, we heard others of the club approaching. Not wishing to look too suspect, we decided to hide behind a green curtain at the end of the building, part of the essential equipment for privatising. We managed to keep quiet but were alarmed when one of the intruders asked what might be behind the screen. One suggested it may be toilets which seemed to satisfy them to leave us undisturbed. Thinking I had got away with the incident quite well, by the next week all had been revealed, for I am sure the girl got more from bragging to the others than I did, although I was sure they were a little envious of such a drama.

Of all the girls, I found Melba seemed to make the most impact on me, for it developed into a regular good-night, at Surrey Road. My name became linked with hers to the extent that at the close of an evening, another girl picked a quarrel with me which ended with the hardest smack on the face I've had, and in front of Melba, which was very humiliating. I just had to accept it with Melba's sympathetic understanding. We carried on together, folk were beginning to accept we were destined for each other. My family had accepted her for tea on alternate Sundays, my brothers' girls would sympathise with me if it was my turn to sit at Melba's table with a much younger family to muck about, and to say good-night in the hall, somewhat disturbed by the giggles of two younger sisters that had gone to bed a little earlier. None of which added to my desire to be alone with Melba. We got on so well that I suggested we spend a holiday together; we drove down to Devon and stayed at various boarding-houses. We loved to swim; Melba would wear shorts during the day and look most attractive. On one occasion I rowed a boat along the coast to a little bay strewn with large rocks. I remembered to pull the boat well up or we could have been marooned. We were able to shelter behind the rocks to change into our swim-suits, without being observed. The time spent together alone was heaven itself, and with due modesty relevant to that age, we assisted to dry each other; nothing seemed to spoil such a time together as I rowed the little boat back to civilisation.

We returned home happy at being together and seeing more of each other. Our future seemed set. The time came for my younger brother to ask me to be his best man and that they wished Melba to be a bridesmaid. The wedding took place the week before war broke out, and I well recall one of the speeches included "I suppose Jack and Melba will be the next". We were not even engaged. My future was now very uncertain, from that time on life changed. Fellows were leaving for the forces, folk moved away, children were being evacuated. We certainly kept together, even after I joined my corp at Aldershot I made arrangements for her to stay for the weekend. I also made a journey to meet her in London, but our association fell apart when I was sent overseas and was forced to live life only for the day. The break allowed Melba to find a partner and marry quite happily.

Some years after I returned home, she made it her wish to come and meet me and have a chat over all that had taken place. I had developed a life of acceptance to remain free to do whatever came my way. My family and friends seemed to be far more concerned that I should marry and settle down than I was. For there were plenty of girls brought to my attention, and although I must admit it all formed pleasure, nothing ever clicked to desire permanent way of life, until you read in another chapter of my visit to Surrey, and that is where my irresponsible romance met its permanent fixture.

WAR YEARS

The war having commenced September 1939, it was not until
the following June that I received orders to present myself to an
army depot in East Ham for medical and 'first preference' of
corp to be enlisted in. I loved driving so tried to persuade the
officers to draft me into service corp, then I returned to my
daily work to forget it until they called me. It was an odd time,
for it seemed to have no future just to live from day to day. I
was informed my medical was A1, and that contrary to what I
thought my employment was not essential so one just waited for
something to happen. I was determined not to attach myself to
any particular girl, least of all contemplate adding to my
unknown responsibility by getting married, even though I was
twenty-nine years old.

The bombing of London had started. War was brought a
little nearer to our homes, with reports of casualities and
buildings flattened by the odd bombs. Our first indication of a
raid was to hear a flight of Spitfires roar up from Hornchurch
Aerodrome some two miles away, then the siren would
inevitably follow. I well recall one clear sunny morning
standing with others in the garden watching our fighters zoom
in and out of the German bombers, and later read the
'playcard' ten for two as a cricket score.

After a long stay in the cellar one Saturday afternoon in
August 1940, guns, bombs and planes had given us good
reason to believe some were less lucky than we. I came up when
the 'All Clear' was sounded to pick up a buff envelope from the
mat marked OHMS, addressed to me! I was shocked at first,
then came the feeling of revenge for all that we were putting up

61

with, after all, I was young and fit and free, why not me, and from that moment on I never looked back apart from realizing the burden I would leave with my father and brother to carry on the business with so depleted staff.

The news soon got around that another fellow I knew had received the same order and a free rail ticket to Fleet, Hampshire, the training depot of the Royal Army Medical Corp. Not quite what I had wanted, yet there was no option. I arranged a simple farewell party for family and a few friends. It was Fleet the next day. I met my mate and chatted on the train journey of all we might expect and arrived early afternoon. Outside the station we met with very many fellows of similar age, but all sorts, some smartly dressed and others looking about as untidy and sloppy as one would not wish normally to associate with. We all agreed the army made a good first impression for we were boarded into hired coaches and taken to the barracks. We had no sooner entered the gates when we were ordered out, "Get over there all whose names begin with A-K, 'A-Coy'; L-Z, 'B-Coy'; you're in the army now." As if we had not already realized it. A corporal gave us a brief pep talk reminding us we were not allowed outside the camp, only under order, and a few more dos and don'ts. We were then handed a pint china mug, enamel plate, knife, fork and spoon, and taken along to the dining-hall to be seated at long bare wooden tables, apart from lumps of marmalade and tea sloppings. I recall I was willing to accept things as they were for we had only just arrived. Perhaps things would improve tomorrow, which as it happened by then I, with others, had geared myself to accept anything they did or said. As the day passed we were left in no doubt that the NCOs knew all, and we shower of rookies knew nothing. It was their way to reduce us to a docile, homesick and thoroughly dejected lot of 'just numbers'. Mine was 7385700 Pte West, almost like a branding iron on you, for better or worse. We were allotted an iron bed in a long wooden hut, six of which formed a 'spider' with one common ablution room. There were twenty-four of us, twelve each side, with our name card on the wall above. The corporal had a separate bunk attached outside our room. His greatest delight was to get up half an hour earlier than the bugle boys called us, and upon the first blast he would open the door, appear immaculately dressed, strut up and down the rows of beds with his cane under his arm bawling "Come on lads, show a leg, the sun's scorching your eyes out."

The peace of the night had passed, up and off to the ablution, try and feel a shave, no lights, for there were no black-out shutters. A good breakfast, no thought now about a big mug or bare table, for we were hungry. Still in civvy clothes we were able to assess each other. The second or third day we were paraded outside the QM store, sized up by the staff and to catch whatever was thrown at us — boots, cap, socks, shirts, battledress, overcoat, and told to get away and return dressed as best we could. It was obvious we looked like a lot of scarecrows, some too big, some too small, some just carrying on their arms. We were looked over by the depot tailor who would say, "Change that man for a twelve battledress, or try an eight shoe." The second parade was a lot better, except for one or two outsize. He promised to make up a suit, and they were able to hang on to their civvy clothes whilst we were given brown paper and string to parcel our civvies for posting back home. I responded with great sentiment, hoping that I would someday wear them again. I had great difficulty to understand how a little cockney chap in the next bed was offering his shoes for sale. I can't remember if he sold them.

Although we were now in uniform it was some days before we became part of it. I did not like battledress, it was certainly serviceable, but appeared very sloppy compared with the officers' uniform. Although we were not allowed outside the camp, friends or relations could visit weekends. On the following Sunday a runner was sent from the guardroom to seek out Pte West, and inform him friends were waiting to meet him at the gate. My brother had driven my mother and father, also my friend's wife down to see us. My first reaction was good! but as I passed the full-length mirror at the end of our room I caught sight of myself in uniform, I felt every bit a convict being visited in prison. No, I can't face them, but then with a great effort I knew I could not disappoint them. Full of emotion I boldly made my way to meet them. I felt so odd to them. I could not speak until we drove well away from the camp, when I had resumed a normal composure.

The next day we were on the parade-ground for marching

and I was singled out as a corner man, which bore some evidence that my corporal had noticed me, for I did enjoy the drill. The coy. sgt. major would stand aside to watch the many squads progress under the corporal's instruction. We greatly annoyed him on one occasion when the order was given "About Turn", half the squad not hearing the order continued marching on and that must have looked very odd to the sgt. major. As the days passed it all became acceptable.

As a preparation of the possible German invasion, for several days we were taken out to the surrounding countryside, marched through a farm barn to pick up either a pick, shovel or fork, it did not matter. With possibly two hundred men now with the tools, under and officer's instructions we were to level out the surplus soil which had been dug out by an excavator to form tank-traps. For several days we worked and were well fed with large sandwiches and soup, then to return back to camp for dinner in the evening.

It was autumn, grand weather, Battle of Britain at its height. Now we were allowed out of the barracks. Prior to joining up, I was very friendly with Madame Olga, a florist in the town, who also ran a dancing school with some very smart young girls that I had met. Word had now reached me that they had been booked to entertain the troops at Aldershot and that they hoped I would be there. I was, and during the evening, Eileen, of whom I knew and liked quite well, sorted me out under a spotlight to sit on my lap and kiss me, to receive all the catcalls from the fellows who I am sure were envious.

The guardroom had a system where you had to book out and then in, always 'properly dressed', and it could work that you booked out 2.00 p.m. Saturday afternoon, return in at 5.00 p.m. intending to go out again, but later decide to stay in barracks. However late, one should have booked back in. One such night I lay fast asleep to be woken about midnight by a guardroom runner, to tell me if I did not dress and report to book in, I would be reported absent without leave. The unwelcomed performance was hindered by the black-out but eventually I returned to find my empty bed, counted six down, not so! until I rechecked to find I was in the wrong hut. I never repeated that silly act again.

One just had to read daily orders, for all sorts of detail — West

700 Dental Parade or inoculation. I had never been
vaccinated, so I took it rather badly. On my arm was a wound
which resembled a large strawberry, and was so painful that
one morning I felt so ill I did not intend to get up until my
corporal told me I just had to, even if it meant crawling on to
the sick parade, which eventually I had to do, with about
twenty other chaps known as the sick, lame and lazy. I was not
one to bluff. I felt so weak I just rolled over and within seconds I
heard, ''Fall in two men, stretcher, take him to the sick-bay,''
where I was well treated and after a day or two, returned to
normal duties.

By this time our sgt. major had been looking through our
enlisting papers to discover that I was a funeral director. This
rather intrigued him to call me to his office for a chat. Did my
work bring me in touch with carpentry? If so he wished me to
make some black-out screens, and so I agreed to try and oblige
him with the hope it might help me in some way. I remember
making some attempt at the job from which he found another,
to build a bar in the officers' mess. They supplied the wood and
gave me a mate. Some weeks later and as it appeared at least
another month before any chance to return home, I suggested
and was granted a weekend pass home to gather some special
moulding and polish, very acceptable. I was able to put my
civvy clothes on again for folk to say ''I thought you were in the
army'' or if I were in uniform ''I didn't know you were in the
army''.

After I had completed my three month training period and
obtained the basic status as third male nurse, the acceptable
qualification for any further promotion, I was taken on to the
depot staff as a storeman, still a private working with one other
pte., corporal, a sgt., and the QMS. I did enjoy issuing out the
kit to the new intake of civilians that arrived each month,
possibly two hundred. We would take a lorry to ordnance
dept., and draw the required clothing and equipment and
return any surplus. We kept a ledger of our stock which the
QMS made sure balanced, apart from a stock surplus he was
well aware of. The quartermaster himself, a Major Galley, was
also an 'old sweat' and he ordered a thorough check, that he
intended to make his own 'spot check'. We were given two
days' notice to arrange all the garments neatly in bundles of ten.

E

It was then our QMS confided in us to load our surplus loot into the forward shelf of a Luton van we used, and make sure it was well out of the depot all day during the QM check only to be returned later. All went well.

I continued quite happy with the work obtaining one week's leave every three months. There was little to do at home apart from working with the firm that I enjoyed.

On one occasion another fellow and myself had heard how it was possible to reach London, without being held at Waterloo Station by military police, without leave passes. One Saturday afternoon we seated ourselves very comfortably in an Aldershot and District Coach with many others on the same stunt. I had arranged to meet Melba in Westminster. All went well, we were nearing London on the Great West Road, when the coach pulled over into a lay-by only to see the biggest shower of redcaps ever, manning five or six tables to record particulars of the offenders. We sat quite still until one boarded the coach and yelled ''All yous that ain't got passes, out.'' We had little option but to give up names and numbers and told to beat it back to barracks or we would be picked up and taken back.

As we walked to find the nearest station, which was Hounslow, we decided it was worth the risk to try a quiet station near Westminster, and so we arrived unobserved at St. James Park, spent a happy time with Melba and returned to barracks later. Sure enough, within a couple of days, my QMS sent for me and asked why I had been so silly, for the 'Charge of Out of Bounds' was out of his hands, and that I would have to answer before my CO, who I am sure had been briefed as to my good service to the store. He admonished me, sort of probation pinned to the conduct sheet and after a time discarded.

Life in the depot rolled on a mixture of discipline and freedom. One Saturday afternoon a fellow a little younger than I challenged me to swim the full length of Dogmasfield Lake. We swam up the centre together and both agreed to see if we could return, and we did, only to crawl out and lay on the bank like a couple of wrung out dishcloths. After an hour sunbathing we made for the church hall in Fleet, and enjoyed the church canteen 'special', six or eight tomato sandwiches.

I had my motor bike with me in the barracks which gave me some freedom, even to take a mate out with me at times. Motor bike gear never suited the guardroom, for upon every return it meant a visit first to my room and check over in the mirror to save a shout of ''Improperly Dressed'' from the sgt. in charge of the guardroom.

During this time the war seemed to be succeeding in North Africa while England was working very hard to prepare for the 'second front'. We in the depot jobs had no illusions that the day would dawn when all us A1 fellows would be drafted into action. Sure enough my QMS called me into his office to tell me of my posting for overseas draft, thanked me, wished me well and advised me to rekit myself with new from the store (I did).

Now still a private, to collect a rail ticket to Leeds, it was a round and about journey until I walked out of Leeds Station in black-out, and as instructed boarded a tram for Harehill Road and reported to the company officer who told me to 'kip down in an empty house, 257 Harehill Road, for the night'. I pushed open the unlocked door and entered a room in semi-darkness to observe about ten fellows all laid out in the floor. ''We're full up in here mate, try the other rooms.'' With full kit I wandered into each room with the same result, finally ending up in the attic exhausted, to drop down and try and get some sleep. After a while I was woken by another fellow who had trodden the same path. We had been instructed to parade 7.00 a.m. for roll call in some nearby church hall. The corporal had a hurricane lamp to read roll. Then for breakfast we followed each other to the tables. Every nineteenth and twentieth man was detailed to collect porridge and bacon from the cookhouse. Being one of the unfortunate I soon returned to the table with the porridge container plus a long-handled ladle which somehow got caught up as to tip the porridge all down my new battledress suit. When the fellows began to laugh it was too much for me, I just cleared off and told them to get their own. I went without and cleaned myself up, and realised what a poor start I had made for my first day in Leeds.

It turned out we had about six weeks to get ourselves prepared for overseas. It was now near Christmas time 1942. We continued to live in empty houses, picture rails and wallpaper ripped off to prevent the bugs from hiding. We filled our palliasses with straw from a cellar nearby and made what comfort we could. We dined in nissen huts near the company office. Our officers tried to remind us it was Christmas Day with some turkey. The orderly officer opened the door at the end, enquired if we had enough beer, wished us a Happy Christmas, and closed the door, which reminded me of 'shutting the hens up at night'. Fortunately for us we were invited out for the evening with friends of the local Methodist Church, for after church some Sunday evenings a mate of mine would sing in the drawing-room of some very nice houses, so we were able to remain human, apart from our very raw army experience at Leeds.

We had to parade each day to check no one had escaped and then given various duties, potato peeling, clearing up, etc. We were also checked and rechecked for teeth, eyes, general fitness, drill, lecture, kit, etc., and given a draft number to which our relatives could post mail, just prior to departure. At twelve o'clock at night, mid January, while Leeds slept, we were marched to the tram depot, transported to the main line station, and boarded a train for Liverpool. We were marched straight onto a ship *The Siberjac*, a Dutch boat, led down a few decks until we realized we were below water, it was the baggage hole which had been prepared with mess decks and forms, only to find we were to share it with a lot of slitty eyed Malaysian young fellows wearing battledress and Pioneer Corps flashes. We were the Medical Corps! This can't be right, and our rejection was brought to the notice of the OC troops who gave us a lecture, we had just got to lump it as part of our effort, so 'shut up'. We did and sure enough that prejudice soon left us and we almost got to like them, for they were students, speaking good English, going out to help our men find their way around Burma and beyond.

The only place one could call their own was the seat you sat on at the table and the shelf which held your kitbag above, and that had to be locked or you could lose from it. On the mess deck you could write, read or play cards. At the end was a rack to hold all the hammocks. We were instructed to take one, put name on it, fix it to the ceiling hooks when we decided to retire. The whole idea went wrong when fellows grabbed their position early on, only to block out the light to the tables. The order went out next day, no hammocks to be pitched before 10.00 p.m.

It was winter but I never felt cold. There was a wet mist when we left Liverpool for the Clyde to join our convoy. All seemed to be a lot of hanging about, not knowing when or where we were going or if ever we would get there, let alone return. We just lived one day at a time as we journeyed out into the Atlantic to avoid U-boats off the French coast.

For days there was no check on your mates, many were just laying around the doors and toilets with seasickness, no desire to eat. After a while we left our convoy for the Mediterranean and journeyed alone down the West Coast of Africa into the tropics. Two or three thousand young fellows, fit and A1, lay about the decks in shorts and vests only. What a sight we must have looked. We were now in calmer seas, blue skies all day, and very hot, which all put us in the mood to enjoy crossing the line (the equator). We were permitted to climb the rigging to get the best view of 'Father Neptune' and the 'Lord High Barber' performing on the open deck on which the crew had erected a large canvas bath. The OC troops was seated on a chair in front of the bath, lathered with a whitewash brush and shaved with a large wooden razor, then to the delight of us all, tipped into the bath. One or two other important personnel followed the same fate. We were all very hot and only wore PT shorts, and then the inevitable happened, the three inch hose-pipe with enormous pressure was directed upon us. We were down like a shot in that pool with the golden opportunity to duck and tip each other over, including our NCOs who just had to take it, until it became too mad and they let the water out over the deck, and our fun was over. Afterwards we were handed a certificate to prove we had 'crossed' the line, one of the occasions when war seemed very remote and our officer almost human.

I well recall the morning, entering Cape Town Harbour, and seeing that fine view of Table Mountain I had pictured in my school geography book.

As our ship glided alongside its moorings, most of us made for the port side, if only to catch a glimpse of the ATS girls who were driving the port officials alongside. Such an attraction caused an enormous displacement of body weight, experiencing enough list to tip the ship up. My own fears were soon confirmed, when the ship's emergency whistle was blown

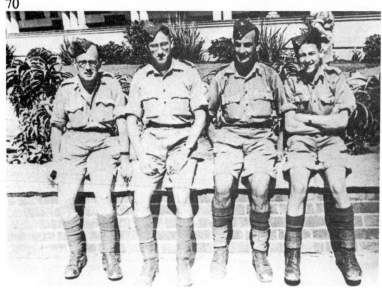

With my three mates, arriving in Cape Town, S.A.
Privates Walsh, Almond and Bert Holloway

for 'Action Stations' to direct the weight more evenly across the deck. When we felt it had righted itself, we were told to be patient, for shore leave would be operative within a couple of hours. The excitement was great, with so long at sea. After a pep talk on how to behave ourselves, we were issued with passes and a condom to save bringing back any infection on the ship.

During the voyage I had worked with three other chaps of our corps, in the ship's hospital. We walked off together, soon to be met by a real mature South African woman who introduced herself as Aunty Crongi, "You look the kind of boys who would appreciate a visit to my apartment for a nice cup of tea." After the stuff our palates had been reduced to on the ship it was a temptation. It all appeared genuine, so we accepted and followed her to her comfy home and enjoyed three cups of tea. She also offered to get in touch with our folk at home as one of our fellows was anxious to hear if his wife had delivered the baby he had ordered, and that all was well. As we stayed in Cape Town for a few weeks, he returned to hear the good news he had hoped for. All the time we continued to write home, but receiving no reply, as it was all coded to army box number we knew not where.

During our stay I was given a hospital job, although billeted at the Base Reinforcement Camp in tents. I had set times as a ward nursing orderly that gave me one free night and the whole of the following day, this was a lonely freedom. I found I could call at the YMCA in Cape Town for a shower and a chat with other fellows, and for one shilling, a bed on the wide landing, with possibly twenty more fellows, to wake up for a 'full house' breakfast of bacon and eggs etc. Then I would take a long train journey out to some remote place, only to return to the same old hospital job, thinking of home, of which I had heard nothing for over two months.

A day came when we were ordered to board another ship, to we knew not where, but after a few days at sea we put into Durban, some said we had engine trouble but our officer knew full well, it was another arranged pause, where we were to stay for another six weeks. It was a lovely resort but the beaches were covered with barbed wire. We all continued to feel very fit and to a large extent enjoyed life. We attended and made friends with the local Methodist Church folk. With two or three of our fellows, I visited the lido, after a swim we sat at a table, feeling quite generous I ventured across to the refreshment hut, to return with a tray of tea and cakes. When suddenly a sky hawk swooped down and grabbed the cakes. One can feel a fool with both hands holding the tray. We knew better next time.

The days passed quite quickly until the time came for us to again board a ship to we knew not where. We had really enjoyed South Africa and the welcome we received, for there may well be worse to come. Ours was not to reason why. We had not been treated so well for nothing, for unknown to us we were crossing the Indian Ocean to land at Bombay. It was now into May and still we had heard nothing from home since January, except that England continued to be bombed. We spent a few days in a base camp with hundreds of tents, all the same; it was hard to find the exact tent we called our own. A day came when our drafts were sorted out, and about one hundred RAMC men put on a train for Deolali, our corp's own base unit. We were welcomed by our own fellows at the camp, allotted a bed in a tent and in a short time, handed a large pack of mail for each of us. Some received a hundred letters. When I was handed sixty-three, the emotion was so great, I gripped that bundle not knowing what it might tell me. I was scared! After a time, I decided to open the last date first — if all was well at home, I could read all the incidentals at leisure, and fortunately it was so, to provide my mind and heart with the peace I so greatly needed.

Our new surroundings were very primitive; mainly tented accommodation, bullock carts for transport, and a dirty bazaar the only organised life outside the camp, a very rough place after South Africa. For a bath, one would select a crude wooded cubicle, with a large round galvanized bath. You called a 'Bisty' to bring the water, one hot and two cold in cleaned oil cans, wired together and carried on a yoke over his shoulders, plus a long handled scrubbing brush if needed. The beds were called 'charpoys', a rough wooden frame that supported the rope base for the 'durri' or sleeping mat.

After a few days to get settled in, I was sent for by the adjutant, who had read of my experience at the English depot store. He explained to me that he had just returned from Burma with the Fourteenth Army to find the stores in a mess, he wondered if I would be the chap to help him right it, and get the ledgers correct with the stock. I was instructed to visit the store with him the next day. I found only two privates in charge, one O'Neil that I found to be very co-operative and a good clerk to help with the ledgers. Many items were missing and a surplus of such things we had never heard of.

Most of my other mates were posted toward Burma, various hospitals and field ambulances. The adjutant explained that he could not give me promotion yet, but gave me his full authority to run the QM store. The journey to the ordnance store was at Nasik, too far for the bullock carts, and so the army engaged a contractor for lorries, which were poorly maintained. On one occasion I found myself some twenty miles away with a broken-down lorry and no food, and not the least hope of getting any European food. For the first time I accepted to share a meal with Brahman, a clean high caste young chap, he offered me a chapati to dip into his bowl, I remember it was a small amount but very sustaining.

O'Neil and I told the driver we were very disappointed with the poor state of the lorry, only to receive a reply a few days later, to say in his best broken English "Bor Sarb" (his governor) "wished us to take wine with him". We never accepted such form of bribe, that was the way they ran their business.

Among our responsibilities was the care of the officers' cases and trunks handed in to the base store when they were ordered into active service, they included their personal belongings, and sports equipment etc.; from time to time we would be instructed to pack them up to return to the UK, if the officer had retired or died. A day came when O'Neil and I were moved to a brick built store. I looked after the equipment and next door O'Neil would look after the trunks, we could speak over a dividing wall.

We still had to use mosquito nets over our rough wooden beds, and after a while we had reason to complain to the quartermaster that we were frequently disturbed by rats running across the beds during the night, to which he was able to get us a trap. We worked out that the ideal bait would be of the 'iron ration' we had in the store, Bovril and chocolate. It was hard to believe but the first night I set it, I got out of bed five times to dispose of dead rats and reload, then gave up to get some sleep. Mosquitoes could be heard buzzing around the net, but what proved the worse were bugs; sitting at my desk wearing just shorts they would crawl out of the chair joints, to bite. It would mean holding the chair over the chimney of our oil lamp, to burn them out, or to take off my pith helmet, turn the lining out, to find the same offenders. Worse was yet to come, all the men were complaining that their beds were bug ridden and the biting would disturb their sleep. Reporting this to the QM, he had no doubt how to deal with it, "Order a bug bath from ordnance." Sure enough an enormous iron tank arrived approx. seven foot by four foot, and we set it up then lit a fire under it to boil it full of water. One by one the fellows brought their wooden beds to be debugged, it worked and it stunk!

Most of my time was spent down on the plains in the Bombay Province, shorts and shirts were the order every day, early morning a warm pullover, it was the only time cool enough to play rugby. One could always be certain of the weather of cloudless skies, for the monsoons were always preceded by high winds for a couple of days.

Around the camp was a very deep ditch some twenty feet wide and the same depth 'The Nulla' as it was called, most time there was just a trickle of water until the rains came and filled it to the top in a few hours. The staff at the depot operated to sort out and issue kit to fellows posted to all parts of India, various hospitals and field ambulances over a vast range of climate. We did receive a reprimand from a CO for issuing a party of men to arrive in freezing temperatures with only shorts and shirts. I think we only made the mistake once.

There were about sixty men working together, some office, catering and stores. I was now given the rank of lance-corporal. Even the CO would respect the store and asked if he required a change. As on one occasion he did require a new respirator case, while doing so I discovered a tin of corned beef, he told me it was an essential part of his equipment, henceforth I took his advice.

We all worked well together almost isolated, one hundred miles from Bombay. Twelve months had passed without even seeing a white woman. An undesirable state, we asked our officers if we could have some kind of break. After a while they arranged for a dance with the company of some twenty ATS Anglo-Indian girls from a hospital a few miles away, and we had to send transport to collect them. It was not successful for they were only interested in the senior ranks. The general atmosphere was so low, it was never repeated. By now I was promoted to the rank of sergeant. We again appealed to our officers even for a train journey to Kallyan some fifty miles away. This was refused as the town was too dirty and out of bounds to British troops. Finally with a mate I was given a pass to spend a weekend in Bombay, what a thrill, even the train journey. We arrived at the station and were directed to the British Services Canteen where we were welcomed by a few English women, possibly officers' wives or of civil servants. After some refreshment offered they asked if they could do anything for us, darning or repairs. I am sure they never realized just what we had received just talking to them, after not seeing a white woman for so long. It was the enjoyable break we needed, without taking advantage of all a city like Bombay had to offer to the love-starved troops.

Returning to the depot very refreshed from the break, our CO asked if we would prepare ourselves to collect about one dozen raw Indian Army recruits, and make use of them to replace more of our men to go forward. O'Neil and I agreed to give every assistance as this was a QM dept. job. The evening came when my Corporal O'Neil reported he had returned with the men and settled them in a tent for the night, and told us of his experience of collecting, two from one tent and two from another, as if he were selecting various breeds of chickens. None could speak English, but he had a list of their names and castes (trade). In the morning I accompanied the quartermaster to meet them, they appeared almost frightened. As we called their names 'Vasa Andy', 'Karmila' and so on, we were able to receive a faint smile of recognition to their names, which enabled us to place them to various duties within the camp; sweepers, water carriers and washermen etc. We were left with one odd one, very much younger, Krishnan Nair, a bright good-looking young fellow of eighteen of the tailor caste, much higher than the rest, so we decided to take him into the store with us. He responded so well to pick up English and our ways

With my Indian Squad, Deolali, India — 1943

that the adjutant claimed him for his batman.

Our job included to drill them and generally encourage them to work, this was not an easy task, they would have been far happier in loin cloth than battledress and boots. We enjoyed training them. It pleased our officers to see they could replace more trained men to go forward. We would march them in squad form to their 'pictures' in the bazaar, and altogether they responded very well. When one returned from his leave down in Southern India with a very large pineapple especially for me I realized that they were appreciating what we were doing for them.

Two years had passed since we arrived and we had kept up letters that gave a mind picture of life back home. One could imagine the excitement hearing a month's leave back to the UK was being arranged. As this was being affected by the length of Indian service it was a few months before I handed over my store keys and boarded a ship, *The Monarch of Bermuda*, for Liverpool next stop. We were now routed via the Suez Canal, and although recently reopened, it had not been sufficiently dredged. We were stuck aground until a tug arrived from Aden to pull us out, then on again. As we neared England we could obtain their radio news to hear that the German Army was collapsing, and by the day we reached Liverpool we were handed an English newspaper with the headline 'German Army yields to Monty', what a welcome home.

We quickly devoured a special English dinner of roast pork, and boarded a fast train, direct to London, still concealing a huge bunch of bananas for the fruit-starved family. Home again! what a welcome to be offered by any and everybody. One felt proud to be in uniform and positioned with thousands of others outside the palace demanding to see the King and Queen and Winston. There were many street teas that followed. Folk felt so relaxed and happy and generous towards each other. The weeks soon passed with a faint hope they would not need to drag us all that way back to India, but not so, Europe yes, but Japan had still got a lot of army in Burma and beyond, and it was Britain's intention to give India to the Indians not Japan.

So back we went to settle down again when the home leave seemed like a dream for the war effort was as real as ever.

Although I was not to take over my old job, I was offered certain jobs that required travels. The most memorable was to escort an English fellow that had been kept in gaol in Madras. With two privates we set off on the long journey, two days on a train with a change at Secunderabad for several hours. We left the station at Madras by rickshaw, a form of human taxi, and was handed over quite a docile fellow who gave us no trouble to return back to barracks; it was a wonderful experience right across India. After a while my CO sent for me to have a chat about peace celebration in the UK, and went on to say that in consideration of all I had done for the depot stores they were going to offer me promotion to warrant-officer, but it would mean moving on to another unit and I could have my pick just where I would like to go. I suggested if he thought so well of me I would leave it to him to decide where he felt I would be capable to hold such a rank.

The day soon followed to find myself sitting in a train bound for Bhopal, a military hospital some few hundred miles north. As I sat on my own, trying to adjust myself to my new rank, a staff sergeant sitting opposite me addressed me as ''Sir'', it was not easy to conceal the fact that the previous day I was only a sergeant, for I found he was bound for the same posting as myself.

On arriving at the hospital I was quite well received with two pieces of major advice, first to look after the matron who would frequently parade the grounds with her red parasol, and was master of all she surveyed. Also to spend at least one evening a week with the men and be prepared to lose a few rupees at their 'Housey-Housey' or bingo as we called it; I did both. As for the matron, I had to accompany her at eleven o'clock each morning on a tour of inspection of the general hygiene, drains etc. If all was satisfactory the rest of the day was free, but it was very hot, mostly resting. A lot of the patients were Italian prisoners, sent over from the North Africa conflict. One I found was an artist in civil life, he most generously offered to paint me a picture of my choice if I could find him some paints, which I eventually found in the bazaar; I settled on something spiritual, 'Behold the Man' upon a piece of old tent canvas. He made up a tube by soldering small tins together, which I was able to bring home in my kitbag — a real treasure.

After a few more months we were told of the effect the atom bomb had caused to change the whole course of the war. Devastation as no doubt it was, had it not been used, I am certain many of us would never have returned. It was the lesser of two evils I am sure. After that the war seemed to peter out, with rumour of repatriation. All warrant-officers were offered a commission of captain if they were willing to stay on for one year to escort our wounded men back to Australia on a hospital ship. Although I was very tempted, I declined, recalling how much my father needed a break back home, for I knew he was carrying on as much for me as himself.

It was December 1945 back home again in England to receive my discharge papers. As I was handed my conduct sheet the officer observed "A clean sheet West, but quite a few pin holes," where I had been dealt merciful probation only, no conviction. I received a civvy suit, trilby hat and a shirt I would never wear, along with a whole bundle of advice on 'How to settle down again in Civil Life', a far more difficult job than I had imagined.

SETTLING DOWN

Many of my set were married with children. They were not the same people as me. I declined to join the British Legion, or my corps association, or even collect my service medals. I don't know why, except I suppose I wished to forget all about it and get back to where I left off. I tried hard to regain my interest in the Methodist Church, and started a youth club for boys, with two other ex-service fellows. We took them to camp at Stapleford Abbots, fresh with our army experience, we all agreed it was a real success. As for my church activities, I was greatly encouraged by a new Minister, Rev Trevor Dyer, for he had seen war service as I had; together we made quite a headway.

Now still living at home with my parents, I was never short of girls, and Betty, my father's secretary, attracted me quite a lot, for she accepted to accompany me if my parents were away. I was happy to receive such attention from her, although it presented no future on my part. I felt at times I could well settle for a life of freedom and unattached, except that my parents were always hoping I would eventually find the right girl and settle down to as happy a married life as they enjoyed. Looking back, I now feel my minister friend must have shared their view, for he offered me an invitation to spend a weekend away with him at friends, in one of the lovely parts of Surrey. At first I hesitated, then as if a premonition had struck me, I said "Yes, where?" And he told me of some sincere friends of his, a Mr and Mrs Mann with their son Ralph, for all he had told them of me, would dearly like to entertain me for a weekend. I did fear a little, for just what I had let myself in for, but I became excited at the abrupt effect it would have upon my humdrum life, of trying to 'settle down again' for the past two or three years.

It was now autumn and a pleasant Saturday afternoon when I drove my friend down to Surrey. On our arrival we received a most friendly welcome and shown to a room I was to share with my minister friend of about the same age and army experience. We enjoyed a delightful evening touring around Box Hill and Dorking, to return back for supper. After which we spent a short time together in family prayer, led by Mr Mann (a deacon at the local Baptist Church). I just accepted this as part of their way of life, that I would be able to endure. But gradually I felt a real deep sense of peace, almost as John Wesley had experienced. On retiring I wanted to tell my friend all my innermost thoughts, my hopes and fears, which lasted well on into the night. When I awoke I was able to find life did have a purpose, my mind seemed refreshed. We all went to church on the Sunday, and on returning after the evening service, I enjoyed their customary event to sing favourite hymns around the piano, with Mrs Mann and several of the young folk from the church. Then to bed and return home in the morning.

I wrote to thank my host and hostess, for all the weekend had meant to me. After a few months I received a further invitation, which was equally enjoyable. It was on about my fourth visit that Mr and Mrs Mann suggested we accepted an invitation for Sunday tea, with their church friends the Prismalls, a mile or two along the road into Kennel Lane. I drove the four of us to be greeted by a charming lady, whose husband although a little deaf, gave us a most cordial welcome. It was when seated at the beautifully arranged table that I discovered that Ralph and I were sitting opposite their two daughters, both very delightfully happy, although very much younger than I. They gave the appearance that they were well trained to keep their place, so I kept mine, for I had no wish to spoil what was to be a very happy tea party. After a few hours together and strolling around their large garden, I left with my friends, and then to bed. The next morning, Bank Holiday Monday, after breakfast I sat to watch Mrs Mann making apple turnovers for the young people's picnic, when the conversation got around to the Prismall's reaction and especially Daphne's impression, that she had made known to her mother. I conceitedly accepted the flattery, and in consequence offered if Mr and Mrs Prismall would like to, we could all drive out to meet the young members, directed by Mr Mann, for he had arranged to take tea at Leith Hill. I willingly joined in the group snap and was able to obtain a copy in a noncommittal way, for they were a jolly fine crowd of young folk. The next day I returned home and tried to dismiss the whole experience as another happy weekend, until I received, this time, an invitation to spend a whole day with the Prismalls.

On arriving, their welcome included their ninety-year-old grandfather with whom I enjoyed conversation. After dinner I suggested that Daphne, the eldest daughter, accompany me to explore more of the country lanes, we decided to stay for a while, where we could be alone together. It was then we were able to share our thoughts and to find out just where we had arrived in our lives. Two hours passed all too quickly, only to leave us eager to spend more time together. The next day, back home, where nobody knew and if they did they would never understand. Letters expressing each other's thoughts developed into a cause we were determined to plan together, yet could it really be that this was the girl, born eighteen years after myself, could really mean all she hoped in me. Could I choose this girl and state and keep all the marriage vows I would be called upon to make, if I wanted her for my own. Such doubts that flooded my mind were hard to dismiss, and yet we continued to meet in the beauty of the Surrey countryside. We spent many hours in the woods, so secluded, to explore each other's minds. I would often suggest 'no white man had ever been so deep in the woods before'. Even after the sun had set and the owls began to hoot, we would scramble back to find the car and speed our way back home to be reminded 'you are very late' or that they were worried about us, for ten or ten-thirty was the accepted time to return to such a household.

We continued quite happy together. When Christmas came with the inevitable 'family pull' I decided to split myself, first with Daphne, and to return home for dinner with my own family. As I left in the early morning to say goodbye at the gate, I suggested to Daphne that when she went back indoors she looked under the cushion on the settee and if what she found was not quite what she had expected, at least it would be a deposit. She later wrote to thank me for her gold watch, and all it meant to her. We shared alternate weekends, Dagenham v Surrey. Working in a bank at Guildford, we got to know Waterloo Station very well.

For some odd reason I decided to meet my old friend Mrs Mann, shopping in London. She had a great love for Daphne and tried to convince me I had a treasure and expressed her surprise that I had not given her a ring. This was a big step for me, I never wished to hurt Daphne in any way. Soon after I began to gain the assurance that I was on the right course and feeling she would do her part to prove me right, we found ourselves looking in jewellers' windows; Daphne had expressed the wish that I chose the ring. After giving me some ideas, I made the choice and decided to place it on her finger on Easter Saturday 24th March 1951. Not being entirely aware of all the excitement the evening would generate among her family and friends, I arrived at her home as usual late afternoon, to stay for the weekend. I spent the first two hours with the family, retaining my own excitement for when we could be alone; it appeared afterwards I had caused some concern as to whether I had changed my mind, or forgotten the ring. As the evening drew on and the birds had gone to sleep, we drove out to a favourite spot, overhung with beech trees, in a lay-by that had witnessed many a kiss and a cuddle at the end of the day. I switched off the lights and fondled her left hand in the quietness of the evening, full up with ample love and emotion. Daphne implored me to switch on the interior light, that she may see what was to symbolize the contract from that moment forward, to make our lives one. After exclaiming her admiration for all it meant to her we decided to return to reality and share our joy with others and receive the good wishes and cards previously sent in anticipation of the event. We were engaged! The course was set to spend the succeeding months to plan a wedding, where to live, furniture etc.

Some months previous I had acted as best man to a friend, of whom I asked "How do you make a start on this job?"

To which he replied "Just tell her mother and you will be half-way there!"

Sure enough Daphne's mother proved a masterpeice at such organising. All I had to do was give my opinion when asked, and turn up with Ralph, my best man at the appropriate time and place — Saturday 1st September 1951 — 2.00 p.m. — Fetcham Parish Church, with all my family and officiated by the Rev Drinkwater of Little Bookam, followed by a grand reception in the Barn Hall. After a happy and exciting send-off we left to spend two very happy weeks in Torquay. Then to return with such added support, to fulfill all my hopes and dreams for a successful future.

BECONTREE CEMETERY

Soon after I returned from the army to work with my firm, my father told me of a visit he had had from a firm of accountants in London. Acting on behalf of the Becontree Cemetery, they had told him how they were responsible for their accounting, free of charge. It was owned and controlled by the Church Property Trust, and they were concerned for it was losing money. At their suggestion they wanted us to consider to offer for the freehold, and take it off their hands. After a while they made a further approach, of which I considered with my father, for we were taking by far the greater amount of funerals there, and that was no more than two or three a week. It was suggested they were considering an offer in the region of one thousand pounds. The whole idea of being responsible for a cemetery at any price, required a great deal of thought, as to just what we were letting ourselves in for. After some weeks had passed we had hints that one of our competitors was showing an interest. I responded by seeking a meeting with the accountants at their Cannon Street offices in London. They laid the whole project before me and appeared very keen to push a deal through. My immediate reaction was to offer a lower bid, to take or leave, a figure of four hundred and fifty pounds, which they hesitated to accept, but would willingly put my bid before the trustees. Sure enough after a week or two, they accepted my offer, but with a condition that we placed a collecting box for their charity prominently within the chapel. When I revisited the accountants to pay the deposit I rejected any strings attached, which they accepted. I then formed a company with a capital of five hundred pounds to include the setting up costs.

Then gave my father a share of fifty pounds, also to my brothers and sister and left the remaining two hundred and fifty shares for myself. My brother-in-law agreed to look after the secretarial and accounting side.

We started off quite well, but after a few weeks the sole employee whom we had inherited as the grave digger, reminded me he had been kept on very low wages and now hoped that I would consider an increase. After doing my best to explain the income did not hardly permit it, he promptly retorted "Put the prices up". When I told him we would then lose work, he made his point by proving to me the economics were such, that one less grave to dig per week, would give him more time to improve the appearance of the grounds. Therefore folk would choose to avail themselves of our particular cemetery, and so that was the road to success. Income did increase to assure us of a reasonable profit and a drastic improvement in the whole place, we were able to build toilets and a brick built shelter (that still remains).

On one occasion I was called to inspect damage done by horses that had roamed in and around the graves. The boundary was enclosed more by banks of earth than fences, which would have been costly to erect. There was no electricity laid on. The roadway up called 'The Chase' was only gravel which needed continual repair, for it was full of puddles in the winter, and very dusty in the summer.

Within the cemetery there was a special plot laid out with wooden crosses marking the graves of the German airmen brought down during the war, for which we were responsible to the War Grave Commission to keep neat and tidy. The war had concluded some four years earlier to when we were approached by a representative of the German Embassy with the hope we would permit them to arrange a Memorial Service on a Sunday to follow the English Service of Remembrance. After confirming with the Home Office, we were told it was permissible, but to be kept in 'low key'. The afternoon arrived when we received about fifty German cars with their families from the embassy, and then for their Ambassador himself Herr Von Haworth, to arrive in his chauffeur driven Mercedes limousine. His diplomatic courtesy extended to show his appreciation of our co-operation to look after the graves of their

With the German Ambassador Herr Hans Von Haworth — Last visit 1960

people. The whole afternoon was a very moving experience for all concerned. We continued the annual service for a few years, until they arranged for their disinterment, to be reinterred with many others in a central cemetery in England.

By now I felt we had done much to restore the cemetery to be quite well accepted by the community. On one occasion while chatting with the town clerk, he informed me his council would be very interested to acquire the cemetery if I would be willing to consider such a proposal. I did condescend to invite an offer for the freehold which turned out to be so mean I ignored it completely, for we were not anxious to part with it, although I had felt at times it was demanding, both in capital and planning, as was my own firm. My father was beginning to leave more to myself, although I would add he was keen to help with any ideas of expansion I would put up.

A year later when in conversation with the town clerk, he reminded me they were still interested and this time I should name my price. After very much consideration of the thought of trying to run two big concerns, calling out for expansion, I could well end up without making a success of either, and so we agreed to offer for a sum in excess of ten times what we had paid for it, and even that was reasonable for them to make a quick decision. We handed over all the relevant documents and plans. After receiving the cheque which was divided among the shareholders, we disbanded the company of Becontree Cemetery Limited, tinged with some regret.

ACQUIRING PROPERTY

There were times when I longed to rid our yard of all the building plant and supplies. Large racks of scaffold poles and timber I felt spoiled our approach to the funeral directors' side of the business. My opportunity came when I spoke to a friend who owned a small plot directly opposite where a pair of old cottages had been demolished. He offered me the plot for just over £100, for no buildings would be permitted as it would be required for road widening within a few years. We moved most of the unsightly plant and timber across the road. We were able to greatly improve our frontal appearance, although our one office had to serve both our building clients and our bereaved families to arrange funerals.

A few hundred yards along the same side, was an old wheelwright and undertaker's house and yard. The business was practically non-existent, apart from a few sheds with lettings for car storage. Mr Howsego was well over eighty when he asked if I could act as his executor and finally clear up when he died. The brewery owned the freehold and when eventually it came to my lot to settle up his estate and hand the property back, I asked if they had anything in mind for its use, as I was sure my brother would be pleased to make use of it for a nominal rent. After some consideration they agreed we should demolish the old house, and make what use we could of the sheds and yard. We lost no time in transferring all the building side of our firm, to leave our sheds and office free for the funeral requirements.

Although my father agreed with the change he still liked the building side, for he had started his working life with a very rigid apprenticeship with Mr Coe, and between them had built some very fine houses to their credit. By 1950 Mr Coe had died leaving my father as sole trader; we were mainly funeral directors. I made several appeals to him to give up the builder's side, which was to a large extent being subsidised and even holding back further expansion. After my marriage I made a final appeal, suggesting my brother was given building business and be offered a limited subsidy if he needed it to help him along. He again refused purely through sentiment, which although I understood, I could not agree, in consequence I decided to go on strike, refusing to help him with any work that came in. After two weeks, when I felt as unhappy as he, my father suggested we should 'have a chat about things', which resulted in him entering into a partnership with me, and giving the building side to 'C. J. West' whilst we retained the original name of West & Coe as funeral directors. We visited the solicitors and revised the National Westminster Bank Acc. Romford 1903, and we were in business. With all now on a firm footing, we worked hard to make quite a good profit in the first year. My share was used to purchase my financial interests in the new company.

Within the next year we were faced with the renewal of our branch shop lease, for we had been at Lodge Avenue for twenty-one years. We were not doing too well, 'Woodcocks' had opened at Parsloes Avenue, and were sharing work with us. The Co-op were attracting families with their dividends. We were also reminded that the rent would be increased. It took considerable courage, but we decided to give it up and return to base and concentrate to give the best possible service from the village. It was now 1958 and we began to increase our numbers. With the private chapel of rest built within our garden, we felt equal to our competitors.

As time went on I decided to ask the Woodcocks if they would be interested in an offer for their Parsloes Avenue branch, but was declined, intimating that they would bear it in mind if that position presented itself in the future. Some three or four years later I was called to the telephone as Mr Woodcock was hoping to speak to me, and he enquired whether we were still interested in taking over his Parsloes Avenue business. It certainly came as a shock to be dealt with fairly promptly. My father accompanied me on the first round of talks, when we agreed in principle to have the necessary documents drawn up. It seemed quite a reasonable offer that we were willing to accept, and to move in within a few weeks.

Our volume of work increased by about two or three each week. One of our employees took up residence and served the firm very well with the help of his very able wife as receptionist. Previous to this impact, we had been successful in having purchased all the land rented from the brewery, which included two cottages, that we were able to link up with our own White House site, commanding quite a large frontage on the Rainham Road presenting all the ground we needed to develop a modern funeral establishment. My brother's business was now largely taken up with our expansion and maintenance work.

After a few years, unfortunately we were thrown off course by a large council redevelopment plan, to include the whole of our land and business. We tried hard to fight off their compulsory purchase bid, but when it became inevitable, we engaged our surveyors to demand the best price possible. We were somewhat satisfied when a figure of around sixty thousand pounds was agreed, however this included our old home The White House. This was not only a sad blow, but left us in the difficult position of finding alternate accommodation to carry on the business. We certainly had the money, but nothing seemed to present itself, until one day Daphne told me of something she had heard, which suggested the owner of a grocery shop was in very severe financial difficulties. I took it upon myself to engage our agents to make some discreet enquiries as to obtaining the freehold. The shop was quite near and was served by an access road for cars. Time dragged on so I called in and made some pertinent enquiries as to the exact position. I was told that things were bad and that she never owned the freehold, also the lease was held by the bank securing a loan of one thousand pounds. The owner of the property had offered to sell, but she never had the money. Within a few days I had checked out to find it had been sold two weeks earlier to an investment company. With some smart help from my solicitors, I was able to track down the Congress Investment Company of Brighton, I suggested to them that the tenant would like to purchase, but was under great difficulty, although she had found a friend who was willing to help her, if they would be good enough to part with the freehold. After some hesitation they agreed, at a figure we were quite willing to pay, about four thousand pounds to which we had to add the bank loan. During the time of transaction I had to lend further cash and even help to stock the shop to save a bankruptcy order being served which would have disrupted the whole deal.

The day came when after making a few alterations to include a chapel of rest and a smart granite shop front, we were able to move our entire business to 630 Rainham Road South on the opposite side of the road. This was now 1966, and we had not been there long, before we attempted to buy our neighbour's shop, but were refused. We allowed the former leaseholder to remain in the flat above, as our caretaker.

Now quite settled to control the number of increasing funerals from our Parsloes Avenue branch, I realized we were being invited into Rainham village a lot, and that there was no established funeral firm there; this prompted me to seek a shop. After spending quite a time finding suitable premises, I eventually decided to check out an end shop in the broadway. I found the shopkeeper interested to the extent he gave me a figure he would require for the lease, but wanted me to buy his stock of wool, nightdresses and knickers, all stuff I never wished to be responsible for. I also had to reaccommodate him, for I needed the flat above for our receptionist, and it so happened I had a tenant who vacated a cottage in the village, this he accepted. After holding a sale for all his junk, we moved into Rainham to carry out some alterations; chapel etc.

A few years later I contacted the baker next door, and offered to take over sheds and bakehouses etc., that were left derelict. There were stables with iron mangers, the brick built ovens to remove from the bakehouse, also a flour loft to make use of. We had reached 1972, it was about this time that Jeremy was able to help his uncle, and gain an interest in the firm's procedure, for he had left school, but attended a day release course on business management. My brother and Jeremy worked hard to knock the whole property into a useful unit, where we were able to store and make the majority of coffins that we required.

Soon after we had settled down at Rainham, word reached us that one of our main competitors was seeking offers for his business; Mr Butler had developed a heart condition that prompted him to take life easier. Although we were in direct competition with him, we had both acted fair, which enabled him to accept an invitation to have a chat. He handed me his last three years' balance sheets to look in to, which included four shop properties, Hornchurch, Broad Street, Green Lanes and also West Ham. I made it clear that I was not in the least bit interested in extending my business any further into London. Although the firm did not appear to have made a great profit, I was offered the three properties for the figure his agents had recently valued them at, plus motor vehicles, stock and something for the goodwill of the business. A deal something in excess of sixty thousand pounds, which seemed quite acceptable to both of us.

We formed a separate company and although Mr Butler agreed to continue for a time, it was his wish I found an understudy. Looking within my own staff, I had Mike my very competent secretary and Peter Bookey, manager of Rainham branch and Terry Newman who had worked at head office and proved himself very loyal and straightforward, so I agreed to transfer him to work under Mr Butler with due tolerance, until we felt he was able to accept full responsibility of managing director, an appointment he has served exceptionally well.

In 1975 the owner of the Parsloes Avenue shop made an offer to us of the lease for eight thousand pounds, that we willingly accepted as a good investment. In the same year we were beginning to assemble a small fleet of funeral cars, and so we decided to bring the Butler's Hornchurch shop with its large garage into our own firm, for a cost of five hundred pounds, the goodwill, for I already owned the freehold within the Butler deal as with Broad Street and Green Lane shops.

About this time we had heard that Gilderson Funeral Directors of Seven Kings and Ilford were seeking offers for their business. Through the years we had much car hire from them, which built up quite a friendship, so that I was able to invite 'Mr Leslie' to talk with me at 'Peerage'. All seemed very cordial, but at the time he was in no position to give me figures.

Rather than waste time, I decided to engage a surveyor to help me make an offer, which I did, and to hear suggestions from folk that we were about to take over, then to my utter disappointment, we heard they had disposed of it to another firm without coming back to talk with us. I never gained full satisfaction for such unwarranted behaviour, but I contended it smelt a little of a 'Masonic act' that I had never been attracted to in any of my deals.

Nevertheless our business was continuing to increase so that we had just *got* to enlarge our head office, to maintain our efficiency. Therefore I made a much larger offer to my neighbour, I was again refused. It was in sheer desperation that I asked my cousin, who was running a DIY shop and yard almost adjoining our block, only to find he had sold his lease a few weeks previously, yet he willingly gave me the new tenant's address, also the owner. I wrote to 'Imanuel' who replied he would consider, if he could find another place suitable to him. Eventually he decided to stay on, to at least see the two remaining years on the lease out. It was then I approached the owner, Mrs Lee, who lived on the west side of London and seeked her interest to sell. She did reply by asking if I would make an offer, to which I made a guess of twenty thousand pounds. Mrs Lee arranged to visit 'Peerage' for afternoon tea, and talk it over, which resulted in her willingness to let us have it for the price we offered.

Having now the trump card in my hand, my agent wrote to my new tenant for rent, and a list of certain dilapidations within the terms of the lease. Mr Imanuel's immediate response was to seek a meeting with me, to which he gave me a slap on the back, and said, "My wife thinks I'm clever but I've got to hand it to you now. Here are all my papers and what I paid for it, pay me that and give me something for my trouble and the lot is yours." All went through well, the freehold and the lease were mine.

I wasted no time in engaging a surveyor to tell me what I was letting myself in for, to make alterations to the shop, also to include a private chapel of rest. His report came back that it was not a good building and said "Knowing you, Mr West, my advice would be to demolish and start again." I had bargained to spend a possible thirty thousand pounds, but to completely rebuild could cost three or four times as much. Although such a figure alarmed me, I mustered a certain amount of bluff, when I asked my 'young bloods' to help me design all that we would require as a modern purpose-built funeral home. After a couple of hours on the lounge floor we formed a block plan, with the help of Lego bricks. I took it to my brother-in-law, who put it on the drawing-board, then took it straight to the planning department of our borough council, demanding to know if they would help me, for I was confident it would be an asset to the borough; they had no mortuary facilities themselves. I am pleased to say they did help us.

Before we demolished the old building, we were sought out by an advertising company to erect hoarding to enclose the open front, offering quite a considerable sum in rent. Within a few weeks of the site being cleared, we received a very tempting offer of one hundred thousand pounds for the site, but we stuck to our intentions to build. Time seemed to drag with the official architect that we arranged a meeting with a builder that had shown a keenness to build for us. An afternoon together with Jeremy, I decided to place a large amount of trust in Peter Wright of WT UK Construction Company, who offered to build what we had planned for approximately one hundred and forty thousand pounds. We worked well together, it only needed the official architect to see our constructural plans through the council. Phase (1) was the main building — Phase (2) to be completed the following year, was the store sheds and garage for our fleet of seven large funeral cars, estimated at a further forty thousand pounds. We got on so well, and somehow were able to find the money without too much effort, that we decided to complete the whole unit by 1982.

The date coincided with my mother's birthday, a memorable date to me, for I bought my first car on the 17th October, also we opened our first branch shop on the 17th October; in consequence I felt it fitting to invite my three brothers and my sister to dinner at 'Peerage' on Sunday 17th October 1982, and to visit the funeral home for a preview in the afternoon. A friend of mine played the organ that I had installed. It was a most impressive occasion, thinking back as a family, over our parents' simple but solid foundation. The official opening was on the following Wednesday in the presence of the mayor, also presidents of the National and London Funeral Association. We were justly proud of how we would now be able to cope with a larger volume of work in comfort and with efficiency.

*   *   *

One fine afternoon I walked into a shop that I had chosen on Aveley high street, to enquire whether they would be interested to dispose of their lease, and was told to talk to the manager at the top of the village, from whom I gained very little help. Some weeks later Jeremy accompanied me to try again and seek out the owner of the lease. This time we met the governor, an older man that seemed somewhat impressed with Jeremy's enthusiasm, for he decided to consult his accountants for a figure we might consider. We haggled a bit when we received it, but finally agreed to meet each other half-way. Then we were able to make alterations and include a chapel of rest, find a receptionist and open to anticipate about one funeral per week. After opening in the early part of 1981, the whole venture has proved very successful even attracting work from Tilbury and Grays.

And 1985 presented the opportunity to purchase the lease of our neighbour's shop in Rainham. It was larger so we were able to include the private chapel within the building and a complete new shop front to conform with the council's idea to keep the Broadway a village. The whole change cost something in excess of twelve thousand pounds, without being able to buy the freehold interests, although it offers a very good service to the town.

*   *   *

For some time I had shown an interest in Frys' Funeral Business in Hornchurch high street. It was owned and managed by Jim, as we knew him. A hard-working honest man, in partnership with his wife, the daughter of the founder. There were no children. He lived a simple life, that I felt for him personally. With my large successful business, we readily accepted any request for help that he needed from time to time. He never appeared to be able to take a holiday, and seemed to find it difficult to plan a retirement. After a chat with him on one occasion, I decided to write, and set out what I felt would give him the chance to retire; that he might let us buy vehicles, stock and freehold, etc., then he could bank the money, and if he preferred to, continue to belong to his clients for as long as he wished. I never asked for a reply, but trusted in due time he would consider my offer, in his own interest as much as mine. Some months passed when I was saddened to learn he had died suddenly. His wife found a friend to help her carry on for a few weeks, but eventually made her way to her solicitor with my letter of offer she had found. We were subsequently sent for and reminded that they would seek other offers to compare, but gave us until the deadline to make our final offer. Understandably now, two larger firms had made offers and also that the business was adjacent to our Hornchurch branch, that gave us an economic advantage and in spite of certain strings attached, we put in a firm offer of one hundred and fifty thousand pounds, which did not include the freehold. The whole deal collapsed when we heard that the widow had accepted a far lower offer from one she had claimed to have known all her life, for she wished to retain the freehold and continue to live there with the minimum of disturbance. We certainly left the deal with some disappointment, but were fully assured under the circumstances, such a firm were more geared to accept the limitations, rather than my own fast expanding modern firm that could never have tolerated opportunities to pass us by.

*   *   *

So much for my business investments all of which were included in my personal estate as 'sole trader', what was far more responsible for my capital growth was the continual investment in tenanted property.

After the war any surplus savings I had would seek to buy cottages, content to receive low rent, with the chance that one day they would become vacant then sell for a profit. Many landlords became unwilling to continue with excessive repairs and receiving a low controlled rent, so that they put them on the market with no idea that within a few years such property would leap with inflation and demand.

I suppose my aunt gave me the first opportunity, to offer a pair of cottages for five hundred pounds, for I soon found that the owner of the adjoining three cottages was willing to part with his. Now with five tenants, I felt quite a landlord and enjoyed collecting the rents. Unfortunately things took a dramatic change when the borough council decided to purchase the whole lot, within a redevelopment scheme. I suppose I was able to treble my money on the deal.

By 1960 I had established a good relationship with a local estate agent, who was willing to offer me such property that came on to the market. In 1964 he was able to give me particulars of a block of five villas, well built, about the turn of the century. The total cost asked was two thousand, five hundred pounds, with which my bank gave me a little assistance. The rents were low and they we in continual need of repairs but fortunately escaped the council's eye for redevelopment. My father owned an adjoining house, that I was able to buy for one thousand pounds some time later.

As the tenants died or vacated the properties, I was able to sell at a considerable profit in line with inflation. Over the period of a few years, one was sold for six thousand, another for eight, another for twelve thousand, another for eighteen, and the last one for twenty-two thousand, which now leaves me with one, in which I have installed a bathroom and is let at thirty pounds per week. That would I am sure, fetch fifty thousand pounds if vacant and brought on to the market. The whole block has added much to my fortune. Even after paying all my capital gains tax demands. Apart from these I was able to purchase a villa in Barking for three thousand and five hundred pounds, with a controlled tenant, who pleaded to buy some years later for fourteen thousand pounds. By 1976 I again accepted the chance to buy a pair of cottages with a lease back for a professional business, for six thousand pounds with an annual rent, now at more than half their cost. There were several more odd properties I have bought and sold at a profit, always adding to my capital growth.

For the first three years of our married life, Daphne and I lived with my parents, sharing their large house. There were several reasons for this besides the difficulty of finding anywhere suitable. It also had the advantage of being able to cover the business calls, as my father and mother were now spending more holidays away.

By 1955 we were able to buy a building plot almost opposite where I had owned my first plot at sixteen years old. The roadway was still unmade by the council. It was a corner plot that would attract larger road surfacing charges, yet the cost was reasonable and I was able to engage a builder to erect a pair of three-bedroomed houses, of which I was able to sell the inside house for £2,000 and kept the outside corner house with the larger garden for ourselves. After all the effort, we were pleased to balance the books to avoid taking out a mortgage. Now with a new house, that coincided with the expectation of our first baby (without exactly planning such perfect timing!), we moved into Aldborough Road and got on quite well with our neighbours.

My father had designed and built a bungalow on his original plot, nearly opposite, and my older brother lived in one of three houses, that I had helped to build, in Manor Road just after the war.

Our garden was large enough for Jeremy to invite his mates to play cricket or table tennis outside on the lawn. It was a very happy time and convenient to attend to the business demands only a few hundred yards away, be it day or night. By the early seventies my father and mother had both died and their bungalow was sold, also my brother had retired and moved to Clacton. It was then I began to listen to those who suggested it would be good policy to invest in a larger house. So in 1976 we decided to look at property in the Emerson Park area of Hornchurch, to come across a small close of seven large type houses. The builders had only just commenced and were reluctant to accept a deposit on the particular plot that we had chosen, but subsequently agreed, offering any variation we required. At this time they were able to add a games' room. We were the first to move in. It was several months before we had any neighbours, for some reason they never sold as quickly as they had hoped. They were offered at £60,000 which was a sure indication that nobody dreamt that their value would leap to £300,000 plus, in little more than ten years, and the fact that such profit of one's own residence attracts no capital gains tax, buying a large type house in 1976 was certainly a very good investment.

Although we had never arranged it, the year coincided with our silver wedding anniversary, to which we invited the whole family to a 'house warming' and silver wedding party combined. Quite apart from the party, Daphne and I decided to return to Daphne's home for the weekend, and relive the events of just where it all started. On the Saturday evening we drove to the same favourite spot that had meant so much to us. The beech trees still overhung the lay-by in that Surrey lane, and as we sat in the car the setting was just the same. Daphne took off her engagement ring to enable me to re-enact all that took place in that same spot, some twenty-five years previously. Under the moonlight of that beautiful September evening we quietly thought over all that we had been able to add to our lives during the past twenty-five years. Accepting the completed chapter with humble gratitude, where better than the church of our marriage on the Sunday morning could we offer our thanks and renew our vows to carry on for as many more years as that will be ours to share.

Through the years we have never been very conscious of our age gap, until the suggestion of retirement, which due to my health, and keen business interest, I was able to carry on until my seventy-fifth birthday, when I had to accept the substantial pension that I had provided for myself, to add to my state pension. My seventy-fifth birthday seemed the occasion to invite the whole family to Peerage Way, of course they all did the accepted thing and brought me a present. But I had agreed with Daphne, I had reached the financial position where I felt I could share a little with my wider family. My brothers and sister in their time, had at least contributed something of what the business had demanded from the family in its earlier years. The previous evening I had sealed three different coloured envelopes, one for my brothers and sister, second for my nephew and nieces and third for the third generation. It gave me great pleasure to include a monetary gift in various amounts. After I cut my cake on the lawn, one by one I called upon my family and explained how happy I was to be able to share a little with them, to evidence the fact that we were a united family held together by our parents' example.

FOUR GENERATIONS

Coppen John West
Born Dagenham, 1854
Died 1910

Edward John West
Born Dagenham, 1878
Died 1969

Edward Jack West
Born Dagenham, 1910

Edward Jeremy West
Born Dagenham, 1956

Although I have never sold any of my business assets I am reminded of their ever increasing value. So far, my personal estate has been one and the same as my business investments. For this reason I have decided that from the 1st January 1988, I would restructure my firm to a limited company, so as to run independent of my personal fortune and to permit my firm to function and expand upon its own resources. In due course I intend to make some family distributions thus possibly avoiding maximum inheritance tax.

HOLIDAYS

After our happy honeymoon spent around Torquay, it was a few years before we were able to go on holiday as a family. Jeremy and Jennifer were born within eleven months of each other and were now capable of toddling on the beach at Bognor. It was a very happy and enjoyable experience that we repeated a second year, staying at the Royal Hotel so near to the beach that Daphne could take them out to enjoy the bright summer morning by 7.00 a.m. I could call to them from my bedroom window. Jeremy became addicted to the trampoline, set up on the sea-wall. Everything was so simple but like so many other families, we enjoyed watching their excitement and attempting to master such freedom.

When they became a little older, I was able to buy a four-berth caravan, which was kept in our yard, that we could just hitch up and go. It needed very little prior arrangement. With my business responsibilities, this gave us opportunities for short breaks, we could even go out after school and cook our tea some twenty miles into the country. Then of course for several years we made it our annual holiday, touring East Anglia and the South Coast, staying on organised camp sites, where they could meet and play with other children. We would sometimes take a cousin to share it with them. They were now becoming quite useful with all that is required with family camping, especially 'hitching up', collecting the containers of fresh water, and shopping at the camp stores. We were so free to travel on, just as we wished.

The next few years we spent an annual two weeks staying at the San Remo Hotel, Torquay. Although we motored around the area a little, they seemed to find ample enjoyment in the pool and the lawns with other children, splashing about in the warm water, for they were now able to swim.

By 1974 Jeremy and Jennifer were well into their teens and with a little help and encouragement of a friend, we arranged to tour the southern half of Norway. I was able to arrange with Olsen Shipping Line to take our car over and find us a farm where we could all stay for a couple of weeks. We drove to Newcastle and endured a very rough journey over, dreading what the return would be. After handing our car over to us, we made for the farm, which we eventually found. The farmer's wife welcomed us as if we were part of her family. We were fed very well, much of the farm's produce including fruit that she had preserved in the cellar store. We all went out horse riding through the forests of mostly pine trees.

We made several journeys up the snow-capped mountains of which the Daimler appeared to enjoy. It was cool in the evening, we would pile a few of their plentiful store of pine logs on an open fire in the corner of the room. The journey home to Harwich was completely different, blue sky, sunshine, and a calm sea all the way.

It was now 1977, from this time on, holidays took a slightly different turn, for both Jeremy and Jennifer were now capable of arranging their own. This left us free to make a trip out to Jamaica, to visit a nephew and his wife who were working in Kingston for his firm. After some twelve hours hung up in the sky, we were welcomed at the airport and driven back to their bungalow. We spent a few days in Kingston, then were able to hire a car and attempt to go right round the island, first the north side, where tourists, what few there were, were well catered for. We were offered a guide to help us climb the Dunn River Falls for which we had to change into swimwear and climb up the rocks against the terrific waterfall. It was great fun to reach the top, and we did. Then to drive on to Montique Bay a very attractive millionaires' resort, with its cloudless blue sky, calm turquoise coloured water and a beach of soft cream sand, all of which invited us to stay for ever. The water was warm and so comforting to lay in.

As we journeyed on around the coast, we accepted the opportunity to 'change' in a special hut provided for would-be bathers. We thought we were alone, until what appeared to be a lot of black balls floating out to sea, soon came around us. We formed the attraction of what turned out to be a troop of Scouts, twelve to fourteen-year-olds. They spoke quite good English, so I was able to tell them of my own interest as a president of our English District of Scouts. We enjoyed them although they were a little overpowering for Daphne. I asked for one to accompany us to show us where the District Commissioner lived. The boy seemed quite keen, we certainly had to trust him, for he led us many miles to a very remote part, to eventually bring us to the steps of the commissioner's bungalow. He had apparently observed us some miles down the hill, and appeared quite concerned who we might be and what we required of him. After making ourselves known we were invited in to enjoy an interesting chat and offered some fresh dessicated coconut and some fruit juice. He gave us a silk national flag and a few addresses, should we require any further help back to Kingston. We journeyed on to enter a village and hearing a succession of bangs I realised my exhaust-pipe had broken. I shut the engine off to think, no AA, no garages! I was at the mercy of a crowd of young fellows, who told me what my trouble was and where I could get help. In all our travelling and dealings we were continually reminded to be suspicious. There was much poverty. Fortunately we accepted the suggestion to follow one of the fellows to well outside the village, where a mate of his would weld the exhaust for us, which he did. We made it a rule to never carry too much money on us, so he did not get quite all he asked for, but we left them good friends.

It was now raining and getting dark as we journeyed on, we could hear little groups of natives walking along. With my window down and my foot poised on the accelerator I tried to enquire if they knew of anywhere for us to stay for the night. They were able to tell us where we were and that they thought we could obtain a night at 'Enden House' which we took to be a normal guest-house. We parked the car in the grounds and entered a very dimly-lit hall and were accepted, and offered some fish soup with little option of any alternative. I was hungry, so was able to take things as they were. With some difficulty we tracked down the boy to show us our room, he led us up a spiral iron staircase, and appeared surprised when we asked for a key. By this time we were tired and prepared to accept anything, strange that it all seemed.

The bed, a four-poster, was enormous and as we looked around to find the bathroom, we felt as though we were looking around an antique shop. Eventually we were able to scramble up onto the huge bed, with our wallets, handbag and any other valuables placed securely under the pillows. We settled down to sleep. We awoke to a bright morning and very relieved to see our car from the window. All we wanted now was to get away from this strange place. The fact that we had little cash was not the only reason we refused to take breakfast. Settling for our night's board, we had an urgent desire to find a bank. While waiting ouside, we met a fellow who turned out to be a missionary eager to tell us much of what we ought to know of the town, and most enthusiastic to tell us we must visit 'Enden House' as it was the original home of the founder of the sugar industry, and how it was all as he had left it, with a very large tapestry on the wall depicting the lot of the slaves that worked there. Now our experience began to fall into place, although a little too late to appreciate it. He then took us to see the raw sugar being sucked off a dirty lorry to be loaded onto ships for refinery at some South American port.

The island's balance of payments was in a very bad way due to much political unrest. One of their main sources of revenue, tourism, was practically non-existent. Their banana crop had failed. Their export of bauxite appeared to be their mainstay. We met a business man who owned a furniture factory, employing quite a few men; all was standing idle for he was not permitted to import any timber that he needed.

My nephew was able to arrange for a visit to meet the leading funeral director in Kingston; we were advised to take a taxi as it was not a desirable area in Kingston to stand about. There was no door as such, for it was very warm, we looked through a wrought iron gate to be observed by the man in charge; he released the catch for us to enter and introduced himself as Mr Isaacs, and that many years ago he had settled there from London. He certainly gave us the impression he had complete control of the island's funeral work, from the very influential to the working natives. He told us that some years previous he had engaged a London firm to install a crematorium for him, the only one on the island.

One evening while touring around we realized we were very low on petrol, there were few garages around and most closed about five o'clock in the evening. We began to panic, but stayed a while for some refreshment by the water's edge at a cafe. They offered trips out in a glass-bottomed boat where one could view the tropical fish in crystal clear water over the coral rocks, and so we were successful to bargain with the fellow to let us have a couple of gallons of petrol, then we partook of his offer which was very exciting. Whatever it cost us we were able to continue our journey.

On Sunday afternoon we drove to the top of a river where one could sit side by side upon a bamboo raft (it resembled a dozen or so twenty-foot long poles fixed together), seated near to the back, leaving room for a boy to work his punt up and down. The river, The Rio Grande, was shallow in places with many twists and turns, overhung with bamboo trees. It seemed very primitive in parts. At one stage we came across a few black boys without any clothes, eager to dive in for the coppers we would care to throw them. After about two hours we had completed the trip to find as pre-arranged, our car had been driven down for us to drive away. The day came all too soon to leave Jamaica, which had turned out to be more of an expedition and exciting experience than an ordinary holiday.

The next few years we have enjoyed cruising with P. & O. *Canberra* or *Sea Princess*, which takes care of so much that we were willing to accept, to travel for the maximum amount of interest and entertainment, with the minimum of effort. We usually arranged a roomy cabin that offers all the facilities one could wish for. We have been able to visit many of the Mediterranean ports, and most of the Baltic capitals.

After a few times one becomes quite confident to partake in all that is offered. For three consecutive years Daphne has spent her birthday at sea, which has prompted me to decorate our cabin and arrange a party to invite the captain, chief engineers and the entertainments' officers with the help of the ship's catering officers. I was also able to pre-arrange with the radio officer to put through birthday greetings from both Jeremy and Jennifer, before Daphne left her bed, all so clever and impressive. I suppose now as I get older it is good to just park all our cases in a cage at Waterloo Station, join the train to Southampton Dock and within an hour of being welcomed on board, the steward has the cases in the cabin to be unpacked and put into the wardrobes.

Sometimes we would take breakfast in bed or up on the deck. The more formal lunch and dinner were served with personal table waiters, in the restaurant where we would join friends in happy conversation. If for any reason there was some objection, the head waiter was on hand to make a switch. We preferred to be seated at a table for six or eight. There was always plenty going on, on the ship. In most ports you could just walk down the gangway, if for some reason the ship lay out of port, they used the lifeboats to ferry across to the land.

*   *   *

Folk would sometimes say, why go abroad when there is so much to see in Britain. This no doubt is true of many, but in our case we have got a fairly good knowledge for we have motor railed to Penzance and stayed at many of the resorts along the Cornish coast. On another occasion we motor railed to Inverness and called at many places in Scotland and through the Lake District and Derbyshire. Having a brother on the west coast of Scotland and son-in-law's family over in Aberdeen on the east, we have made the journey right across the Grampian Mountains several times, in the Daimler. We also made a week's tour of Wales, Brecon and Snowdonia. Completely toured round the Isle of Man and also the Isle of Wight. We also spent a holiday in Oban and drove across the Isle of Mull to Iona, and so I feel we have had our share of visits within our own country, even if it did fail to provide us with sufficient sunshine at the time we most needed it.

FROM UNDERTAKING
TO FUNERAL DIRECTING

Way back in 1896 my father with Mr Harry Coe helped to make coffins as part of the experience within their apprenticeship with George Pearcey, builder and undertaker in Dagenham village. When they qualified they entered into a partnership as West & Coe to commence building houses in Hornchurch, many of which I can still look upon with family pride.

After a few years, they accepted an offer to take over their former employer's well-established business, he was emigrating to Canada. This change added an undertaking section to be dealt with, fortunately 'Old Alf' the coffin maker remained with them. My father took it upon himself to conduct the few funerals that this small village required, even with the help of a wheelwright and undertaker, only a few hundred yards along the same Rainham Road. He personally knew most of the families that would call upon his services. There appeared to be very little profit motive, as it only formed a small part of their business.

In the winter, it was cold and dim in the poorly-lit workshop, for he would bring a special coffin into the scullery room for warmth to finish the polishing. It seems so odd to realize without electric light, possibly a gas mantle would do its best, but it became necessary to hold a candle in one hand and a brush full of polish in the other to paint the side of the coffin; I almost weep to recall the difficulties such as they had to work under.

Even as children we were brought into close contact with the covering and lining of a small child's coffin that was completed in our living-room. Not that we resented it in any way, for we were keen to watch all that took place, for I do not recall any memory of such a job being presented in a morbid way. Such were the foundations of our family firm. We had no telephone, but my father had ample amount of 'runners' for needed messages, which seemed at times a little too frequent.

Most funerals were carried to the church by voluntary men, sometimes engaged by my father, or offered by workmates and family friends. Quite often on a Sunday when the church morning service had finished, which did not always coincide with the exact time that the cortège arrived, yet for economic reasons the men and mourners would not lose a day's pay.

The coffin was always delivered to the home, preferably after dark; I would be given the job of carrying the wooden trestles, sometimes across footpaths, when they would rest it for a while. I can't remember meeting any folk on the way, but gruesome though it may seem, I'm sure it was an accepted thing. A few days later my father would be required to 'dress', white laundered cuffs, stiff collar, on with top hat and frock coat, and present himself as master of ceremonies for the occasion. With the required staff, most distances would require a double, to change over at intervals. The mourners would walk in order of family in pairs to the church, my father leading the way and afterwards lead them back in the same order. He may have received some refreshment, bid his leave, and return to walk home with the wooden trestles over his shoulder.

These were days when men worked hard and hardly expected any great reward, for time was cheap, there was little to do apart from work; for that was the lot of the village undertaker.

The big change came when the London County Council absorbed the whole of Dagenham farmland for houses. I recall my father, with other business men, trying to come to terms with all this vast programme laid out before them in the county newspaper. The village appeared to become a town in a very few years. The impact upon our business was comparatively small, for all were young couples raising their families. It was an abnormally young age group, presenting an equally large amount of children, who unfortunately suffered epidemics of diphtheria and scarlet fever during 1925-1935, this resulted in so many young families experiencing the first heart-break of

Our 1930 Daimler Hearse

loss. At one time we appeared to be burying more children than adults. All sorts of parents would be forced to meet my father and find in him the desired sympathy and understanding, having five children of his own, apart from being known for his love of children. All this pouring out of compassion, built something into the minds of those bereaved, of trust in such a firm as West & Coe, and I suppose that is what formed the foundation of what is known as the firm's 'goodwill' which we have continued to build up through the years, with efficiency and sincerity to arrive at what now almost becomes inestimable. It is always gratifying to read letters of appreciation of our services, which to some extent serves to spur us on to an even better service.

Within a few years of my working within our firm, motor funerals were introduced. Our own carriage master bought a 1930 Daimler hearse, built by Dodderidge Brothers of London. I was quite keen to introduce it to the families, sometimes to receive a rebuke of ''I suppose you want my neighbours to think I am rushing him away'', and so we were content to leave it to the distant funerals to introduce the motors.

At about this time our carriage master had bought a second-hand 'Maxwell' hearse that we would be able to convey coffins on journey removals. An occasion soon arose where a mother pleaded with my father to help her bring her eighteen-year-old son home from the Isle of Wight, where he had died of TB. She had very little money but promised to pay, given time. Previous to the possible use of the newly-acquired motor, it would probably have involved a horse and man and taken them at least two or three days, good enough reason to discourage such a venture. After discussing the possibility with his fellow undertaker, the two governors and myself set off early in the morning. It was before the introduction of windscreen wipers; when we met a lot of rain, the driver produced an apple which he cut in two and rubbed over the glass which seemed to improve his vision. All seemed to go well, we had obtained what we went for, enjoyed a good meal, and returned home around 10 o'clock on a midsummer's evening to receive a hero's welcome. The family and neighbours had gathered in anticipation that her boy was being brought home, all achieved within one day and so economically. I am sure we enjoyed the experience, which saved landing the family with the full expense.

It became very difficult for firms to keep both forms of transport, especially when the horses spent days in their stables. The final parting with horses was a very emotional experience for many undertakers, for they knew their horses and all they were capable of. The change became speeded up during the war for there would be occasions when they would be frightened in the streets at the sound of bombs and guns. The very first motor hearse bodies were somewhat modelled on the horse hearse, mounted on the motor chassis. Through the years they have become streamline to match the follow-on cars.

As staff, we were pleased to move from the old horse-drawn vehicles, on which the coffin bearers would stand on the rear step. In severe winter conditions, such exposure would permit jumping down for a while, to run and regain circulation, then to return while the cortège continued on. The undertaker himself would ride well rugged up beside the driver, to direct him, but on return would invariably stand on the back, all of which hard old customs subsequently gave way to the motor saloon.

In the early days before heaters were introduced, car rugs were provided for the attendant to arrange, when loading the mourning party. The large coach also gave way to mourners becoming more exposed with larger car windows, although at first blinds were fitted, for those who wished to seclude themselves from view.

Arriving at the house with the hearse and a pair of horses, possibly two coaches with pairs, as a young assistant the coachman would hand down the 'velvets' to fix to the harness. This I considered was a decorative form of modesty, for even the best-trained horses had little discretion when and where to carry out their normal functions. The hearse would be decorated with flowers a few lengths from the house, and when all was complete it was customary to invite the coachmen in the house for a 'nip' to keep out the cold. When I would be asked to stand beside the horses' heads, presumably they would then feel 'under orders', the hearse would be drawn up to receive the coffin.

After all the cars were loaded, if ostrich feathers were asked for we would put them on the tops of the hearse as it was considered cruel to place them on the horses' heads. The undertaker would lead and the bearers would walk beside the hearse, customarily carrying truncheons as a symbol of the times when they were used to beat off body snatchers. If it was considered to trot the horses, we would walk alongside the horses, unclip the velvets and throw them up to the coachman. Funeral horses never galloped although there was a temptation to speed things up a bit, if we were running late. Even trotting a distance, could discharge a white lather over their hair; that would not only give the coachman extra work to polish the leather straps, but would also receive a rebuke from other undertakers, for what they would consider undue treatment for their animals.

My early days, before cremation became generally accepted, London cemeteries were very busy places, for it was quite usual to join with four or five other funerals for a communal service. It would require quite a lot of room around the chapel for the carriages to file round in order. Undertakers would be very critical of each other's turnout. At the City of London Cemetery, the funeral that arrived first in the chapel could well be the last out if all others had availed themselves of a private grave and your family had only afforded a public communal grave. Leaving the chapel last would mean often waiting for a parson, after he had gabbled a few committal prayers over the preceding coffins. At Abney Park Cemetery they so valued their ground, that common graves were dug to a depth of twenty feet and over, to receive some ten to twelve coffins within a few days. A space to erect a very small headstone was in great demand that to reserve a head and foot position, I would be instructed to call in the office before leaving the cemetery and then perhaps be disappointed.

*   *   *

Now a word on the old style undertaker and his role. His premises were often very dismal, mostly painted black relieved with gold, and in many cases in the East End of London, his shop window invited all who passed by to observe his men with their white carpenter's aprons, polishing, fitting and lining the ordered coffins, appearing quite proud of their craft and the fact that their services were in demand. He would also hasten to engrave the inscription plate to place promptly in the window that gave those interested to observe the latest departed, and that their particular firm had been entrusted with the arrangements. Seldom was a body left at their premises, although often in very unhygienic surroundings a change over from hospital removal shell to coffin would take place.

The general public attitude to death was steeped in mystery and superstition, and that undertakers themselves were a class of their own, preferably to be avoided until required. While coffins remained at home, all kinds of suggestions were meted out to avoid anything unpleasant. It became quite acceptable to find a pail of carbolic disinfectant placed under the coffin, or a saucer of sliced onions laid on the table. The great change no doubt was prompted when during the last war the whole population were brought very closely in touch with death from air raids, after assisting the removal of those killed to improvised mortuaries. The impact was such that it all became a common topic of conversation, folk surprised themselves, how they managed to deal with such a task. It no doubt cleared

H

our minds of much mystery and superstition to accept that once death has taken place, it has to be dealt with in a practical manner.

Now the time had come for undertakers to become accepted as funeral directors in a more professional approach. One of the first things was hygiene, and to take over the responsibility of preservation while resting before disposal. Embalming became more readily available for all cases if required. The National Association of Funeral Directors embarked on an extensive education course. Firms were encouraged to change the general approach to their premises with the emphasis upon comfort and care for the bereaved families. Funeral directors were also encouraged to select their staff for smarter, cleaner and even younger men as drivers.

I have listened to many who have been responsible for urging the great change over the last few years, and endeavoured to conform strictly to the high code of funeral conduct accepted by the Board of Trade, all of which I was able to model my new funeral home upon, to incorporate all the best in funeral requirements. Thus I have lived through the experience from undertaker to funeral director and now am thankful that I can offer from my firm as good a service as any.

There are far more demands than most folk realize, to deal with families, that irrespective of whether they are rich or poor or of any particular political or religious denomination. Our role is to offer the best advice and meet the common point of the bereaved. In many cases we can handle situations fairly simply, but every now and again we are faced with some tragedy that demands so much more. Dealing with a family often embittered, as in the case of the young girl murdered and hidden from the family for a long time, all so widely reported in the press. With parents to face all, it desires an experienced funeral director to exert every effort to arrange such a funeral to restore the dignity to such an innocent child.

We have to produce a coffin designed to portray the love and value of its contents, co-ordinate all concerned to do their part to finally achieve the full benefit of a well-conducted funeral, completely disregarding any possible financial reward. Such funerals command large attendance and yet there are times of extremely lonely funerals. An elderly lady arranged her husband's funeral and told me she would be the only mourner as her only neighbour would be at work; I decided to ride in the car for companionship, of which her gratitude extended to invite me in for a cup of tea on our return. Hesitating at the time it would take on an oil-stove, she surprised me by thinking to pre-arrange it in a flask, not quite the same, but I was pleased to accept for her sake. There is a lot spoken of elderly people's anxiety to find sufficient money. We as many funeral directors deal very sympathetically by tailoring things down a little, or by showing them where help can be found. I cannot recall ever refusing a call, and if we have cut the cost I am certain we have never cut our quality of service to any family, whatever the circumstances.

I am sure my experiences would not be complete without a mention of one or two of the odd things that occur from time to time. As on one occasion I was asked to pause the cortège outside the factory gate, to receive the respect for a departed workmate. Arriving, I was surprised to find there was not the usual line of men assembled. I carried on to the crematorium where I was met by a fellow funeral director, feeling somewhat guilty. Explaining I had been instructed to pause at the factory gate, I told him I had found nobody about. He then went on to confess, observing maybe they were there for his funeral he paused, which seemed to satisfy them, but unfortunately the director's car had followed and were now attending the wrong funeral. He was sorry but confessed it was too late to do anything about it.

On another occasion I arrived at the office to take over the duties of a member of staff at short notice. From my briefing papers, I arrived at near the address to find a lot of expectant mourners assembled in the front garden a few houses from my address detailed. All so expectant, that I considered they had decided to meet at the alternative address. They were eager to offer me a particular wreath to place on the coffin. Only to turn to view another hearse and two cars approaching, of which the conductor of our other firm appeared most disturbed, as to how it could be that we had commenced to deal with his family. It was with much embarrassment that I had to explain we were not the right firm and gave way for the other firm to take over. By the most exceptional set of circumstances, we then moved on a few doors along, realizing that the two identical cortèges were booked for the same time within a few houses and neither of us were aware. Had we been permitted to have carried on, it would hardly bear thinking about as to how we would have righted the situation.

On a very busy period in the winter, I had set off to Tottenham with a complete cortège, when outside the City of London Cemetery, we discovered the half shaft had broken on the hearse, the thought of a replacment hearse was highly impossible. I could only hope to use the telephone in utter despair. Yet as though I had rubbed my lamp for my guardian angel to present me with an empty hearse, a hearse returning with firm's name-plate, revealed it was returning to Tottenham. Within a few minutes, their staff co-operated to facilitate the transfer for us to continue and arrive only a few minutes late.

One other experience worth a mention was the occasion after the crematorium service had finished. I was about to load my mourners when I caught sight of a fellow who had left the front entrance door, seeing a bus arriving he made a dash across the snow-covered pool, which he had considered was a lawn. Appearing scared and waist deep in the water, I had to quickly consider whether to save his embarrassment by ignoring the situation or which I eventually did, try and offer some comfort. When he asked if there was anywhere he could 'dry out' I feel I could be forgiven at the thought of just how helpful the crematorium staff could be, a blanket was found, when a car driver offered to drive him home to explain all to his wife. Precautions are now taken to prevent any repeat during the snow-covered garden.

PEERAGE WAY AND
PERSONAL INVOLVEMENTS

PEERAGE WAY

We have lived in our large Georgian type house since it was built in 1977. Apart from Daphne and myself it has been an 'open house' for our children and our grandchildren, at any time they wished to visit or stay with us. It has always been our intention to share its comfort. Daphne loves entertaining and arranging all sorts of parties with the help of her large and well-equipped kitchen. Visitors generally find it a home to relax in. It is certainly roomy with five bedrooms, one of which has an *en suite* bathroom and dressing-room, also a guests' bathroom. The hall is quite spacious to enjoy my organ, which I find relaxes me, even if it fails to entertain others. A study is a must to take care of all the business that has to be dealt with from home, apart from serving as a miniature library. The main lounge is panelled and most tastefully decorated, as is the dining-room, so different from our 'family lounge' where the grandchildren are permitted to litter the floor with their toys and at times use the heavy duty suite as a trampoline. On one or two occasions we have removed the furniture from the room to provide seating for some sixty guests to see a special film, or to provide a full breakfast for thirty men with a speaker to follow, and also to hold a whist drive. Before the house was completely built, we were able to arrange with our builder to include a games' room, for which we provided a full size snooker table. This has been a main attraction for many guests. Also on one or two 'final nights' which has brought larger numbers to the table.

I am sure Daphne would never have been so happy without the pleasure to share it with so many friends. We have a lovely garden, only recently I have had to engage a little help. For

117

several years we have held a garden party for our church friends.

When I realize that we very seldom serve any intoxicating drink and discourage smoking, and would certainly frown on any attempt to bring a dog onto our carpets, and yet as Daphne has always maintained, it must be a 'home' not a show house.

After some of our larger parties we have surprised ourselves at how all has reverted back to normal, to leave no trace of all the exciting frivolity that had taken place, a few hours previously. The comfort and security of a well-run home is more appreciated as one's mobility finds its limitation and such is not limited to the size or cost, for I know of many who share the same values within a small bungalow, apart from the opportunity to invite so many at one time.

* * *

INVOLVEMENTS

I feel now it is opportune to reflect upon any community involvements that I have been able to offer myself and my experience. Such desire to serve one's fellow men, I would trace from my father and grandfather who both served as Dagenham Parish councillors in their time. As business men perhaps a little better educated, for the majority of the small population were agricultural labourers, that lived quite honourable lives and made their children respect both men and property. It therefore prompted farmers, business men and others to offer their experience to improve the lot of their fellow inhabitants. Naturally I have had to answer, why, with all my experience of so closely dealing with a complete cross-section of the public for so many years, and apart from my long family background in Dagenham, why I have never offered myself to serve on the local council.

From 1926 all such values changed, for it became accepted that from that time on, such affairs were considered best managed by a political party to push through the new social programme that the huge new LCC estate was requiring, and so some very good experienced men gave way to the party system which sadly included many with very little to offer apart from supporting the party line. All the changes that followed for better or worse were accepted as progress relevant to a modern age.

Local councillorship now denied, I have been somewhat frustrated to observe how narrow such a system works. For the many problems and debates that have directly concerned our business, be it cemetery or crematorium, never at any time has a councillor contacted me for any help or advice with my sixty years of local funeral experience in the borough, or even the fact that I personally owned and controlled the Eastbrook Cemetery for ten years prior to their acquisition. When the local press reported the problems the council were experiencing with regard the cemetery requirements, I with two or three of my executives attended a committee meeting at the town hall, as observers only, at our own invitation. I am sure most folk would have been as surprised and a little upset to have been totally ignored even to the extent to watch the assembled councillors drink their cup of tea, ninety per cent offered nothing to the debate, but just followed the party line put over by the chairman. We left the meeting realizing how pathetic and narrow such a politicial party ran the affairs of their borough. If my presence had received a welcome even without contributing anything, I would have accepted such, but to be totally ignored was a personal affront I had to accept as entirely unwarranted.

Many other ways to serve the community opened up. When our children attended the happy and well-run John Perry School, 1961, I felt more than willing to accept membership on their PTA Committee, and subsequently became their chairman, a privilege I enjoyed to serve along with many other like minded parents. We were able to offer the staff encouragement and raise funds to add a permanent cover to the swimming-pool, that our predecessors had provided.

All too soon my interest was directed to Eastbrook School, which at the time was under the control of a very responsible head with staff of some very fine teachers. With a few other parents we were able to persuade the head to let us form a PTA of which I accepted to become its founder chairman, well armed with my previous experience. We became a very active part of the school and were able to attract many parents who shared our ideals, offering any support for the staff that would help the children and raising funds for the school's welfare.

On one occasion I was approached by a visiting councillor, surprised at the effort and support our association was offering the school asked "Mr West have you ever been offered a governorship?" To which I had to answer "No" for I was assured that those dealing with such 'honours' were somewhat cautious as to my political colour that might clash a little. If this was the only reason, I am sorry for such narrow-mindedness. Fortunately it took the ministry to see the wisdom of a PTA member on the Board of Governors was a very essential contribution, and in consequence my succeeding chairman accepted his invitation to make his contribution to the board.

*   *   *

About this time Jeremy was well into Scouting, and after showing some parental interest and the fact that in my time I was a member of the Scout Movement, I was invited to succeed the mayor as president, a post I felt I had much to offer. I made it my business to publicize the good work being done by so many dedicated leaders, and enjoyed presiding over its annual St. George's Day Dinner, of which the mayor would usually attend.

During this time it was brought to my notice that the lease of the headquarters hut was required by the owners and that an alternative site had been offered, a little more remote than I felt desirable for such a meeting place. I was able to convince the committee that we should look for a more prominent site for the headquarters of Dagenham Scouts.

I started a fund and used my influence to attract others interested to support the idea, and was able to revive the interest of Howard Earl, then in his eighties, for he was the only original Scout of the 1st Dagenham Troop of 1911. Also we received a generous offer of help from an elderly friend I was able to interest. I was very concerned we should, if possible, find a prominent freehold site, however modest the building, we could add as we were able to attract the support, and then all would permanently remain within the cause. It was difficult to persuade the council to let us have sites that we suggested and even more difficult to find a freehold plot, but we were adding to the funds. Quite unbeknown to me the secretary had negotiated with the borough council for a grant or loan, and to my sheer amazement, managed to exclude me from any further knowledge in the project, since finding herself in the position to accept the council's offer. It may sound well except for the fact that in the event of the association running into difficulties, they would be left with nothing, for the council owned the ground.

Feeling very hurt at such treatment of their president, I pressed for details and made several attempts to acquire a balance sheet without success, that I could only deduct that there was never one for me to see just what happened to the fund I had set up. After such an experience, I had to accept the fact that all my interest in Dagenham Scouting had ended when I had felt I had so much to offer.

*   *   *

MY OWN BUSINESS

For the last ten years my business has made increasing demands upon my personal involvement. The volume of funeral orders received have increased every year and the firm generally expanding, all of this, apart from the many opportunities to go the 'extra mile', dealing with bereaved families can be very demanding even to turn out during the night to offer some family a little help and support. As an experienced funeral director I represented my London association as a delegate to the national conference held annually at various hotels of our large cities, possibly contributing something of my experience and ideals, and I am sure receiving knowledge and inspiration from some of the finest men in our calling.

As a chairman of our East London District, many years ago I decided with a few others to offer ourselves for a professional examination and not altogether surprised to be one of the first to receive a diploma in funeral directing, which gave me the opportunity to become a voluntary tutor to various study circles that were set up to gain the coveted diploma.

Although as most trades, procedure is ever changing, but fundamental principles remain. One can only hope to succeed while striving to care and understand to what extent he can help his clients with his experience. To carry out all that is entrusted to him, with a sympathetic efficiency, for so often we receive letters of appreciation to remind us just what our part has contributed towards the therapy, to overcome the loss. All so rewarding, a far cry from the glib remarks hurled at our trade, in the main, by those who have never had to avail themselves of the services of the modern experienced funeral director.

I have enjoyed my work of which I have never wished to have received any great recognition for that which I have been able to do for so many families through those sixty years, continually spurred on by the individual's appreciation either by letter or by word, each day of my life. My greatest comfort is the fact that I have a son so like minded to continue the rewarding work for many of the families I am sure, where I have left my mark. My daughter who has always shown intense interest is only limited for the fact that our work is mainly accepted to be a man's job, fortunately her husband works with Jeremy and enjoys his wife's full support.

*   *   *

There is another involvement that I have enjoyed and I feel it worth a mention. My whole family have always enjoyed gardening, I am sure we are endowed with a horticultural heritage.

My father's uncle and cousins worked a nursery on a commercial basis for many years in Oxlow Lane, prior to the ground being acquired for the large shopping parade. The whole area was covered with glasshouses to produce tomatoes and cucumber that they sold on their stand in Covent Garden Market. I trace my keenness and ability to such influence. The past few years with a little help from seed tray manufacturers and soil companies and the enthusiastic help from Jeremy, we were able to grow over four hundred boxes of bedding plants and enjoy the excitment of selling all so quickly outside the church at Gidea Park. To repeat the sale for two Saturday mornings, we were able to hand twelve hundred pounds towards the church funds, I now find it requires a younger man than I to keep that pace up.

IDEALS REACHED WITH APPRECIATION

At eighteen I was keen to take part in all my Methodist Church offered, attending youth rallies and listening to such enthusiastic leaders as Rev George Allen, who would scream out from the rostrum, to his audience of young people, "Are you Alive? — Oh I know you are breathing, but are you alive to all the opportunites that are around you, and are free for your taking." On another occasion an address "Be Big, Think Big, Act Big, with all your life before you, now is the time! Don't wait until you are too old and spend your last years regretting a wasted life." This was pumped into me as never to forget it. Thanks George!

It was during this time that our district was expanding, Methodist Central Halls were being built to include more of the social side, films and concerts etc. Such buildings were largely financed by the late Joseph Rank, renowned for his highly successful flower milling business, he was also a keen member of the Methodist Church. I well recall a memorable evening, when he arrived in his chauffeur driven Rolls Royce limousine, to open the new Barking Central Hall, of which he had given more than half of the fifty-eight thousand it had cost. I was very impressed that such a wealthy man should come to address the assembled crowd gathered in appreciation. He told us of what it meant to him, to find he had enough and to spare for a cause so dear to his heart, but also of the stress he suffered in deciding the most genuine cases of the many demands made from his purse, a task he finally handed over to his 'Rank's trustees'. One failed to see how the Lord could do otherwise than prosper such a generous man, so willing to return it to His Church.

My young mind seemed to really admire and even envy his life-style, to the extent I thought I would like to pattern my own life on it, for I was sure I had enough years ahead of me to mass a fortune and gain the wisdom, to share some of it with others. From that time I was intent on becoming a millionaire, what a hope! The most money I could call my own at that time, was about one hundred pounds, and half of that was invested in my plot of land. Yet I suppose, compared with others of my age, I was considered well off, and so from that time on meant work and save, to invest in good property deals, to accumulate more capital, for even larger investments. With all my seeking to prosper, I was determined to reach my goal with a clear conscience, all my dealing should be straightforward and honest.

As I found that I could, I would try and be generous and exercise my idea to make a larger gift to some worthy cause, only to experience that something would come my way, to replace that with which I had parted. I never believed a lot in luck, but preferred to rely on what my mother had discovered for me, that I possesed a 'guardian angel' who would see me through some difficult times and certainly console me if I lost a deal, to show me it was no good for me, and then strangely, fresh opportunities would reward me.

I preferred property of which I could see and manage, rather than stocks and shares I never understood. When I made a profit, it would inevitably attract the Inland Revenue, who delighted in pulling me back sixty steps out of every hundred I moved forward. My accountant would advise me to work on what they left me with, and to forget what they claimed.

In 1980 I had to endure a formal Inland Revenue Enquiry, as to just how it was possible to build up so much capital, after paying all my tax dues. It took two to three years to go through every detail of my financial transactions of the previous five years, to search for any tax I had omitted to pay. My accountant finally found a few minor omissions, outside my business activities, that to pay their demand with interest seemed to satisfy their investigations. I now considered I had been purged from such an evil practice! Just whether they felt repaid for their extensive efforts, I am not sure. What I do know is, it cost me ten thousand pounds to receive the thirty page document from my accountants, containing every scrap of my income and expenditure for the previous five years. It certainly was a time-consuming and mind-searching experience, but I put considerable value on the detail within those pages, apart from coining the phrase 'The poor don't realize how well off they are'.

Now casting my mind back over the years, I have tried to discover some of the ingredients that have gone into obtaining or perhaps surpassing my early aspirations and so I have tried to list but a few.

I am sure I owe so much to my parents for so secure an upbringing. My father was a man of very fine principles, as honesty and truth; so well respected within his village. Both he and his father were teetotallers and non-smokers, of which I am sure gave us a pure blood that has never craved for tobacco or alcohol.

In all my dealings and driving, I have been assured of a clear brain. I have also accepted their example to rest from work on the sabbath, to refresh my mind and will. My perfect health and energetic physique was thrown into work and often long hours. When asked what my hobbies were, I had to reply, "Work and after that, more work", although I did do my share of swimming, not that I received any cups or medals.

Another helpful ingredient was the love and encouragement I received from my mother, so devoted to the family and possessing the art of 'ironing out' the many petty differences that arise within a family. She worked very hard for us all, an example we have tried to follow, she lived to see us all happily married, with our families always on hand to rejoice in any successes that came our way. We as a family were given the opportunity to celebrate with them, their Golden and Diamond Jubilee, which gave us the chance to record with real appreciation and admiration, of what their long and successful married life meant to us, their children.

Through my life's story I have acknowledged many folk who have helped me on my way. To those I would add the services of my accountant, surveyor, solicitor and financial adviser, all of whom have helped to keep me in orbit with their professional knowledge, either by piloting my wild ideas through, or advising me against them.

I now come to my most vital ingredient for success, domestic happiness. With Daphne, of whom I could at all times unburden my hopes and fears, successes and failures, and find peace in my heart and mind. To Jeremy and Jennifer with all their returned affection and support in that which I have tried to do. Also to my brothers and sister who have at all times supported me with encouraging interest in the family business that fell to my lot to take on.

Now finally to the Rev George Allen and others, who in my youth urged me not to waste my life, then live to regret it, but to gain the faith to live a full and successful life.

With all humility, I thank God for where I found myself and for the wisdom and peace of mind I continue to receive as I glance back over the seventy-eight years to when that life started.

Peerage Way — Our family home for the last 12 years

Father and Mother — Their complete family and in-laws with my sister and husband and three brothers

My complete family (1988)
Standing: Bill Gillanders, Jeremy; Sitting: Jennifer, Me, Daphne, Sue;
Front: Joanne, Jamie, Clare, Baby Richard